THE MURDERERS

THE
MURDERERS

by
Emanuel Tanay, M.D.

with
Lucy Freeman

THE BOBBS-MERRILL COMPANY, INC.
INDIANAPOLIS / NEW YORK

Copyright © 1976 by Emanuel Tanay and Lucy Freeman

All rights reserved, including the right of reproduction
in whole or in part in any form
Published by the Bobbs-Merrill Company, Inc.
Indianapolis * New York

Designed by Viki Webb
Manufactured in the United States of America

First printing

Library of Congress Cataloging in Publication Data

Tanay, Emanuel.
  The murderers.

  1. Murder. 2. Criminal psychology.
3. Hostility (Psychology) I. Freeman, Lucy.
II. Title.
HV6515.T35   364.1′523′019   76-11627
ISBN 0-672-52158-X

Contents

1

The Roots of Murder

The subject of murder is of interest to most of us. From time immemorial, murder has been with us, starting from the world's first reported family. Much of the best-selling literature of the ages has been based on murder, from Macbeth to the works of Mickey Spillane. Many of our movies and most prime-time television offer tales of murder. The basis of the ever-popular Westerns is the killing of the "bad guys" by the "good guys."

But in contrast to the interest in murder for entertainment purposes, there has been very little interest in homicide as it occurs in reality. Both the scientific community and the public have avoided, by and large, the study of murder.

The fact that people kill people seems to excite little interest in terms of serious inquiry into the causes. We spend billions of dollars on the punishment of murderers, or to pursue murderers, but show almost no curiosity about the phenomenon of murder. We seem to accept it as a fact that people kill, always have and always will.

Any scientific interest in murder is suspect. A number of my psychiatric friends have asked whether, in my own psychoanalysis, I gained insight into the reasons behind my interest in homicide. And frequently, after I have addressed a professional or a lay group on my work with the more than one hundred homicide offenders I have studied over the years, there arises the question as to why I am interested in this morbid subject. If the object of my study were suicide or masturbation, it is not likely I would be asked this question.

I do not know the answer, though one reason may be that I lived in the shadow of legalized murder for five years during the era of Nazi terror. I recall a scene in 1943, when I was fifteen, after having escaped from Poland to Slovakia with my childhood sweetheart Gina, age thirteen, and a boy named Zwi, also thirteen. We were prisoners in an improvised jail which had no lights. The upstairs kitchen had a solitary electric bulb burning. Gina, Zwi, and I, given the assignment to clean the kitchen, enjoyed being in a room with light.

Looking at the lone bulb shining, Zwi said, "Isn't technology wonderful? What a difference one electric bulb can make. If I survive, I will become a scientist."

I remarked, "What's the value of technology if we have to fear for our lives for no apparent reason? If I survive, I will study people."

Zwi survived and became a nuclear physicist at Harvard and at Massachusetts Institute of Technology. Gina survived and became an artist. I went into political science, then psychiatry.

Could this feeling of mine be one of the roots of my interest in murder? I not only have been a potential victim of murder but, in fantasy, killed countless Germans during the Nazi occupation of Europe, though I have never physically hurt another human being. I do not know fully the answer to this question why I became so interested in murder, nor do I think it really requires one. The phenomenon of homicide is a veritable laboratory of human emotions. It should be studied not only for the purpose of preventing human suffering and loss of life but also to expand knowledge of the human mind, particularly the aggressive impulse.

Then, too, a physician cannot avoid dealing with violence, both in others and in himself. Medical practice confronts us with suffering, frustration, and rage. Doctors, regardless of their specialty, take care of people who have been injured or afflicted by disease. And people who suffer, who have been rendered helpless and humiliated by illness, are apt to be violence-prone. Being sick is not only painful but degrading. Illness imposes passivity, which is the breeding ground for violence.

Patients tolerate being asked how often they have sexual relations, or having a finger inserted into their rectum or, if a woman, vagina—interventions that, though necessary to maintain health, are invasions of privacy and stir unconscious reactions of rage against the doctor. What happens to the aggression generated by disease-related suffering and humiliation? One patient of mine returned home after a gall bladder attack. His wife of forty years threatened him verbally, saying he was inadequate as a man and she was going to leave him, as she had often threatened. This time he killed her, feeling more violent than ever because of his illness.

Why is there such a discrepancy between the avid interest in fictional murder and the lack of interest in, almost a universal abhorrence of, the real causes of homicide?

One reason, I believe, is that we don't want to give up the so-called knowledge we already have in exchange for new knowledge that may be more dangerous to our self-esteem. Our image of a murderer, an image we hold dear, is that of an individual far different from us, someone who kills for evil but rational reasons, usually someone who coldbloodedly calculates the carrying out of the horrible act of murder.

How can we reconcile our preoccupation with fictional murder and our avoidance of the study of real murder? The answer is simple and obvious. Our frustrated, murderous wishes are gratified in fiction, where the villain puts into action our secret, hidden wishes to kill those who have hurt us throughout our lives. The killer potential lies in every man.

There are in society three ultimate crimes: cannibalism, incest, and murder. At the present, only the last two have practical significance, for cannibalism is almost extinct except under extreme circumstances, such as described in the recent book *Alive*. The disappearance of cannibalism, except in some remote, primitive tribes throughout the world, cannot be attributed to any vigorous law enforcement, nor to the eloquence of religious and moral leaders. Why have we given up the temptation to eat each other? We have not lost our appetite for meat; there is no biological inhibition against eating people. Cannibalism has become a rarity because the cannibalistic drive has been redirected. We eat other species—cows, chicken, fish—resorting to eating people only in an emergency when other foods run out.

We have been less successful in redirecting our incestuous or murderous drives. The incidence of incest is still quite high, though somewhat lower than murder. Also, the consequences of incest are not as devastating as those of homicide.

Our biggest failure in the socialization of the human animal has been the prevalence of murder. There are many reasons for this. We have never decided to abolish homicide; we merely regulate it. The killing of animals, known as hunting, is regulated by the seasons. This is simple: one may kill deer during a specified time. But when it comes to killing people, a bureaucratic nightmare develops.

The regulations concerning the killing of people are complex and confusing. For example, if your neighbor is in his own house, the principle "love thy neighbor" applies. When he enters your house through the open door as a guest, the principle of "hospitality" applies. But when he comes in through the window, the principle of "defend your home" applies, and you may kill him. But if you kill him when he is leaving your house through the window, the state may kill you for doing this to him.

As a nation we are far behind the times in our understanding of murder. Though murder has been a crime in all societies, probably from the day man drew his first breath, at this point in history we are still applying the same thinking and the same techniques to deal with homicide that were in use thousands of years ago.

There has been no significant innovation introduced into homicide control since the days of Hammurabi. There is no body of knowledge dealing with homicidal behavior as such. Everyone deplores murder, but no one does anything to prevent it. There is no agency or institution concerned with the prevention of murder. I would think the time has come when the problem of killing a human being should be approached in rational fashion. Prevention is the result of comprehension.

One reason we have failed to cope with homicide is that it has been by and large in the domain of the law. We rely exclusively on the penal-legal system to deal with murder. The legal system jealously guards against intrusion and infringement on its territorial rights. Thus the study of murder from a psychiatric standpoint is a neglected area. Psychiatry has entered the field of homicide almost exclusively as the passive handmaiden of the law. Psychiatry tries to supply answers to the legally formed questions of criminal responsibility but neither asks nor answers questions of its own. To paraphrase Clemenceau, murder is too important to be left to lawyers alone.

Psychiatry has avoided the study of murder in spite of Freud's monumental discoveries that show human behavior is determined largely by the unconscious part of the mind and stems from childhood experiences. Freud's findings should have great practical importance and far-reaching theoretical significance when it comes to understanding why a man murders.

Unfortunately, psychiatry and the law are at loggerheads. The law is out for punishment; it does not wish to understand *why* men murder. Criminal law and the trial are designed to fulfill society's psychological need to deny its own murderous impulses as well as to afford indirect gratification of the murderous wishes of all the supposed "innocent."

Murder has been relegated to scientific obscurity by the distorted notion that it represents an isolated, unique form of behavior unrelated to everyday aggression, whereas, psychologically speaking, murder is ubiquitous. It lies in each man's heart when he feels threatened. Murderous wishes, murderous rage and murderous fantasies occur daily in every human being. They are universal, representing the murderous impulses in all of us. This impulse may be either inhibited, displaced, or gratified in a more or less substitute fashion. Murder is not an isolated, unique problem. Murder is the ultimate fulfillment of the aggressive drive in someone driven to the breaking point.

Clinically, this is confirmed by the observation I have made in a number of cases where murderers describe the feeling of peacefulness that comes over them after the completion of the act of murder. This fact is shocking to most people. I know of one murder trial where the calmness and serenity of the accused man set the jury against him.

If we recognize murder as fulfillment of a need (this is not to condone murder but to explain it), then we can better understand why a man murders. We can also understand why our experts have been as loath to study murder as they once were to study sex. There is a parallel in the libidinal drive. The sexual need achieves its fulfillment through the act of intercourse; the aggressive drive achieves its ultimate fulfillment through the act of murder. Therefore murder and intercourse have in common the fact that each represents a direct gratification of a basic drive. Our two most powerful instincts are sexual and aggressive, the ones most dangerous to man, and the power of which he tries to deny.

The denial of murder as an instinctual gratification is shown in our desultory search for the so-called motive for murder. We learn someone has killed for money, for life insurance, for position, for love of a woman. The murder then does not represent a need in itself but merely a means to an end. The police are expected to uncover a motive as part of their collection of evidence. If such a motive is not evident, the public is outraged, speaks of "senseless" murder, or what the Germans call "Lustmord," or pleasure murder. The question arises as to why murder committed for a "specific" reason should be any less shocking than the "senseless" murder. No murder is "senseless." Murder always makes sense in the unconscious part of the mind, where our repressed wishes are stored. The so-called senseless murder threatens the repression of our own murderous wishes and fantasies, and that is why we feel so shocked when we hear of it.

Whenever a murder is committed, a surprise reaction sets in. The act of murder seems to us like a freak occurrence from a strange world. We feel contaminated, and our primary concern is to purify ourselves. A murder trial is such a ritual of purification. The trial aims at reestablishing our disturbed psychic equilibrium: the criminal pays his debt to society, and our own murderous impulses once again are banished from our consciousness. But the price of keeping this perennial purity is to remain in ignorance. Murder, like illegitimate pregnancy, happens most frequently to the innocent and the pure. Illegitimate pregnancy is most common where sexual repression and ignorance are highest. The Australian aborigines, who were not aware of the causal relationship between sexual intercourse and pregnancy, held the lead in illegitimate pregnancies.

We treat murder in similar fashion by attempting to break the causal chain between everyday aggression and murder, unlike our acceptance of the causal chain between the sexual urge and intercourse. The sexually knowledgeable young lady will avoid an overwhelming sexual situation or be properly equipped for it, knowing its physical and psychological dangers. But the aggressively repressed, hostile young man, not realizing the danger of his repressed impulses, will rush into a situation that provokes his rage with a gun in hand, ready for use. The cowboys in the wild west knew enough to leave their guns outside before they sat down to a serious game of poker.

The fact that murderous impulses are part of the human condition might seem self-evident, as witness our many world wars, let alone individual murders, but it is accepted on an intellectual level, not an emotional one. The relationship between the natural, normal feeling of aggression and the act of murder is difficult for most of us to accept.

What murder becomes big news? Not the shooting that occurs in a holdup; this type of murder is received by the public without much excitement. But the murder of a mother by her son, the killing of a child by a parent or a parent by a child, the shooting of a wife or husband—these are the murders that stir our emotions, stimulate our curiosity, and sell newspapers. The "love murder" threatens our repressions and sets into motion our own powerful defenses.

The universality of murderous wishes and fantasies is confirmed by the clinical experience of every psychotherapist. The late Dr. Franz Alexander, who studied the mind of the murderer, said in his book *The Criminal, the Judge and the Public*, "The human being enters the world as a criminal. It is socially not adjusted. During the first few years of his life the human individual preserves his criminality to the fullest degree." And in the unconscious of all of us, the criminal impulses reside until the day we die.

The majority of murderers are not socially abnormal. They share the same social mores and aspire to the same levels of behavior as those who have never murdered. In most cases, murder can be distinguished from such crimes as breaking and entering, forgery, and tax evasion in that it is an *act,* not a *pattern of behavior.* Deviant behavior represents a way of life; the forger, the prostitute, the burglar follow a deviant, not accepted method of adjustment. But murder is generally a nonreflective, impulsive crime. Forgery, prostitution, and burglary would be practically eliminated were the death penalty applied to these crimes, but murder—because of its impulsive nature—cannot be similarly controlled. By the same token, the death penalty would have very little influence on masturbation, an expression of the sexual impulse.

There is another point of difference between homicide and other crimes. In the majority of homicides, one can hardly distinguish between the villain and the victim. Frequently we see the victim as "at fault." What we mean is that he made a contribution to his own demise; in some way he provoked the murderer into killing him. We recognize that the victim and the villain were engaged in a common emotional undertaking.

It is utterly a myth that murder is a crime committed most frequently by hardened criminals who have to be kept in check by stiff penalties like the death sentence or mandatory life imprisonment. The facts do not bear out this myth. The majority of murderers are decent, law-abiding, taxpaying citizens.

In most homicides—between sixty and eighty percent of them—there is an intense emotional relationship between murderer and victim; homicide, so to speak, is most often an affair of the heart. If homicide were primarily an affair of money, bankers would be the most common victims; if it were primarily related to property, rich people would be killed most frequently; if it were primarily related to political differences, assassination would become more of an occupational hazard for every politician. Of course, bankers, rich people, and politicians are murdered at times. But for every banker murdered, thousands of wives are killed by their husbands. There are many more husbands killed by wives than rich people killed by robbers. There are more children killed by their mothers than politicians murdered by assassins. Murder is, indeed, a family affair, because family members both love and hate one another, and the hate, if it becomes excessive, may explode in murder. People invariably kill the ones they love and hate, for no one else is important enough to provoke murderous rage.

Murder is born out of the conflict of hate and love. Murder marks the end, the tragic end, of a very ambivalent relationship. One man went into a rage during a quarrel and beat his wife to death with the butt of his pistol when the gun failed to discharge. He suffered from amnesia afterward. When I told him what had happened, he said, "I couldn't have done that. I love my wife. You don't beat to death what you love." I said, "You love your children, yet you beat them at times." He replied indignantly, "Oh, no. I don't beat them—I whip them. But I love them too." Love and murder are assumed to be mutually exclusive, yet the most superficial examination of homicide records disproves this. The killing in the family is the most frequent one in the annals of murder, as police departments around the world know well. Alfred Hitchcock once said in irony but in truth, "Some of the most exquisite murders have been domestic, performed with tenderness in simple, homey places like the kitchen table or the bathtub. Nothing is more revolting to any sense of decency than the underworld thug who is able to murder anyone—even people to whom he has not been properly introduced."

The image of a murderer carries with it a certain non-specific connotation. It implies someone who is devoid of the human quality of reverence for the life of a fellow being, like a hit man. But in reality, most murderers are more specific than lovers when it comes to the one they kill. As I have pointed out, a murderer usually does not kill at random but picks as a victim a specific person with whom he has an intense love-hate relationship. Outside of this relationship, he is harmless, free of homicidal tendencies.

I recall examining a "killer" at the office of the head nurse of the medical unit of the Wayne County Jail in Detroit. Two deputy sheriffs were assigned to protect me. Before the arrival of the "killer," the officers began clearing the desk of staplers, paperweights, letter openers, explaining that this was a necessary precaution for my protection, since these items could become deadly in murderous hands. I told the officers that the man I was to see, about whom I already possessed considerable information, was harmless as far as I was concerned.

"But, doctor, how can you say that, when he murdered his wife with an ax?" they protested.

"Yes, but I am not his wife," I said.

Another time a dangerous killer was brought to my vacation home in northern Michigan. The prisoner, charged with the first degree murder in a public place of his unfaithful girl friend, arrived chained and handcuffed, according to the regulations. He was held in the maximum-security section of the county jail. Since he lived in a rather sparsely populated county of the Upper Peninsula, he was the only man in this maximum-security section. This meant special twenty-four-hour guards just for him at great expense to the county. The prevailing imagery associated with murder demanded that he be considered highly dangerous. But the elderly sheriff and his elderly deputy who brought the man to my home knew better. On the first day's interview, the sheriff and his deputy watched television in the living room while I interviewed the "dangerous" killer in the separate bedroom wing of my home. The second day the sheriff and his deputy went shopping, leaving the prisoner in the custody of my wife, my two teenage daughters, and myself. The prisoner had not been allowed to shave because "dangerous prisoners" were not permitted to shave by themselves, but since no such restrictions were imposed in my home, he attended to his personal hygiene unsupervised in the privacy of our bathroom. Neither the sheriff nor I was exhibiting negligence or carelessness; we simply knew the person we were dealing with.

Sometimes precautions have to be taken, however, depending on the type of murderer. I recall the case of a young psychopath brought to my office by an elderly sheriff from a well-populated Michigan county. The prisoner was not handcuffed. The sheriff was accompanied by his wife. I left open the door between the waiting room and the examining room and was assured by the sheriff this was not necessary, because "He is a good boy; I have had him for two years; I know him well." I was even more distressed when the sheriff informed me that he was going to visit some of the shops on the first-floor arcade of my office building but that his wife would remain in the waiting room. Noting my puzzled reaction, he assured me his wife was "deputized." I felt rather uncomfortable, since the lady was in her

late fifties and did not appear very agile. The young prisoner fell
into the category of the "non-specific" killer. He had murdered
strangers, and the implications of his good adjustment in the
structured environment of the jail were obviously misunderstood
by the sheriff.

Homicide can be divided into the specific and non-specific
varieties, based on the method of selection of the victim. A
typical example of a non-specific variety is the case of a twenty-
year-old man who spent his childhood and adolescence in public
mental institutions and was psychotic most of his life. At the age
of eighteen, because of legal requirements, he was discharged
from the mental hospital, where he had exhibited some non-
specific homicidal tendencies. In fact, at the age of seven, he was
described by a child psychiatrist as "an uncivilized savage." A
few days after his discharge from the mental hospital, he started
raping and killing women, continuing this non-specific, homicidal
behavior until he was caught two years later. Actually, as in the
case of "in cold blood" described in this book, if there is a study
in depth of the "non-specific" murder, the victim can usually be
shown in some way as having stirred up memories of childhood
experiences that were excessively cruel.

I have studied many individuals who have repeatedly raped
and/or killed, and I have been puzzled by the fact that some of
their victims were left unharmed, or at least not dead. A twenty-
six-year-old married resident of a Canadian town who held a good
job would make periodic visits to Detroit and view pornographic
movies, then develop an uncontrollable desire to rape. He
traveled aimlessly through the streets of Detroit and surrounding
suburbs until he found a woman alone in a car. He followed her to
her destination, then forced her at knifepoint into his car and
raped her. He did this on innumerable occasions over a period of
a few years, at times engaging in such behavior several times a
week. Only on two occasions was a rape prevented by the behavior of the victim. One victim screamed very loudly and he
retreated. Most interesting was the reaction of a young woman he
found in fashionable Grosse Pointe whom he described as very
beautiful but determined. Instead of the compliance he expected,
she scolded him severely, ordered him to sit in her car, and
insisted they talk about his need to rape. She would not let him go

until he promised he would see a psychiatrist, a promise he kept. He commented to me, "Doc, you would not believe it; this broad treated me as if I was a little boy!"

Police agencies throughout the country that issue advice to prospective victims generally recommend compliance with the attacker. I recall being on a panel on crime in front of a few hundred women, sharing the platform with the chief of a special unit of the Detroit Police Department dealing with street crime. He was asked how female victims should react to an attacker on the street. He said, "Give him what he wants if you value your life." The inspector was clearly conceptualizing the attack as the exercise of a well-structured aggression. At times this generalization does apply, but there are rapists whose minds are so disorganized that even the death of their victim is insufficient to end their homicidal rage. I have seen a few cases where the number of stab wounds was in excess of fifty. It was obvious that the attacker continued his aggressive behavior after the victim was no longer alive.

I have also seen a case where a young wife was shot with a submachine gun nearly thirty times. It is not unusual for a forensic pathologist or psychiatrist to encounter cases where six bullets are fired into the head of a victim though the first one most likely was lethal. These are murders that represent disorganized discharges of aggression. The diagnosis and prognosis of an individual who has committed murder depends, I believe, on the assessment of the degree of organization of his mind and the degree of specificity of the particular homicidal behavior. Random selection of victims and disorganized homicidal behavior show severe pathology and a high likelihood of repetition. In this connection, it should be emphasized that it is wrong to assume that an act of murder increases the likelihood of its repetition by the killer. All that can be said is that the act generally affects the probability of its recurrence in either direction—it may decrease or increase chances of recurrence.

Attempted homicide by a criminal might be the end of his dangerous behavior in the particular situation. But attempted homicide by a spouse is not usually the end of the homicidal conflict. It is likely to be followed by a delayed murderous or suicidal act, or psychotic disintegration.

We see then the seemingly paradoxical result of a person who has unsuccessfully attempted murder being more homicidal than the person who has committed murder. Murder can resolve the specific, intolerable conflict, whereas attempted murder may exacerbate it. The intrafamilial conflict is rarely resolved by attempted murder, since the conflict remains unchanged after the attempt and the potential for recurrence is very high. At times, however, attempted murder may on a psychic level represent a completed murder even though no death has occurred.

In the study of homicide, the primary question for a psychiatrist is not why people kill people but why did this particular person kill that particular person at this particular time? In the study of murder, three aspects should be considered: duration of the homicidal behavior, the degree of discrimination in the choice of the victim, and the degree of organization in the mind of the murderer.

Homicide is an episodic discharge of aggression. It occurs in spite of a variety of inhibitory forces. Sometimes the latter can be strong enough to prevent a homicide that is socially approved: for example, in the work of soldiers or policemen.

I recall being consulted by a major metropolitan police force because police officers were missing their human targets at close range even though the officers were excellent marksmen. As a result, the policemen were endangering their lives and the lives of others. This problem is well known to military instructors.

Anthropological and psychological data indicate that there is an almost universal inhibition of the impulse to kill another human being. At the same time, murder appears to be prevalent in all known societies. We then have to understand an interplay of forces which brings about the occurrence of murder. Let us assume that the murderous impulse has gained ascendance and an actual homicidal episode is in progress. What makes the homicidal episode cease? There are four possible causes of termination: external control, sufficient discharge of aggression, reaction of the victim, and death of the victim.

Many episodes of homicidal behavior are terminated by the presence of a controlling force. Frequently the would-be murderer himself invites control. It is not uncommon for an enraged person to entreat, "Hold me or I'll kill him!" The law has recognized this aspect of homicidal behavior in its old test known as the "police-man at the elbow" test. An individual who under such circum-stances did carry out the act of murder was considered insane in the eyes of the law.

Homicidal behavior may cease without bringing about death if the aggression has been spent in homicidal activities short of killing the victim. I recall many cases where the victim survived because the perpetrator exhausted his aggressive resources in inflicting multiple stabbings or blunt-instrument blows. In one case a seventeen-year-old abducted a fifty-five-year-old female university professor whom he raped and then stabbed innumera-ble times, repeatedly saying to his victim, "Why do you take such a long time to die, bitch?" He finally abandoned the victim, still alive, in a deserted field. It is obvious that the more primitive the murderous technique used, the more likely it is to bring about exhaustion of the aggressive energy in the murderer before the death of his victim. Even a sadistic murderer may exhaust his homicidal drive and give up the effort to kill. Two of the most sadistic murderers I have ever encountered described the attempt to kill their victim by choking, beating, or "stamping on her chest," but the woman would not die, and they abandoned her in the woods. Innumerable domestic quarrels constitute actual homicidal episodes that are ended because the aggressive energy has been spent on the victim by the would-be killer prior to the act of murder. As Dr. John Bowlby, the famous British psychia-trist, has said, "No action persists forever. The factors that cause behavior to cease are clearly just as complex as those that cause it to start."

Once the homicidal episode is in progress, the victim is not entirely without control. At times the victim may further stimulate homicidal tendencies, whereas at other times he may end the homicidal behavior. Obviously, here the time element is of cru-cial significance. If the homicidal episode is of very brief duration, the victim has minimal, if any, influence on the outcome. I have encountered on a great many occasions situations where the po-tential victim, confronted with a loaded pistol, behaved in a pro-vocative manner, insuring his own death. In one case, the hus-band, owner of a bar, was counting the money he was about to take to the bank. It was customary for him to carry a loaded pistol when he deposited the money, and this pistol lay on a table near him as he prepared the bank deposit. He had had an ongoing quarrel with his wife, who was eight months pregnant, about her alleged sexual indiscretions. She chose this particular moment, as he made out the deposit in the presence of the loaded gun, to inform him he was not the father of the child they were expecting. He picked up the gun and shot her dead.

In most cases of murder, the homicidal impulse is specific, directed toward a particular person. The death of that person terminates the homicidal behavior, rendering the murderer harmless. There are exceptions to this specificity, as seen in psychotics and in murderers who have prolonged periods of dissociation of the mind.

From the standpoint of homicide prevention, it is of great significance to ask the question: What accounts for the failure to end homicidal behavior prior to the death of the victim (assuming the homicidal episode is already in progress)? Clinical experience and theoretical considerations provide a rather simple and self-evident answer to this question. A highly sophisticated weapon, usually a firearm, shortens the homicidal episode to a point where death becomes the only significant possible cause of termination of the attack. The speed with which the homicidal impulse can be implemented with firearms and the magnitude of destructiveness associated with such weapons render intrapsychic and interpersonal control factors practically inoperative. There is little or no time for reflection if the duration of the homicidal episode is reduced to the few seconds required to pull the trigger. There is also very little reduction of aggressive tension by the actions involved in operating a gun.

The legal definition of homicide makes preventive measures difficult, since it categorizes homicidal behavior according to whether the behavior is "desirable" or "undesirable." This type of classification cannot be used in a preventive approach. Lung cancer and typhoid are both "undesirable" conditions, but they require further differentiation before preventive measures can be instituted.

I approach homicide from the standpoint of a psychiatric clinician, deriving data from the examination of more than one hundred homicide offenders. It is essential to differentiate between conflicts inherent in the characterological structure of an individual and conflicts that are sporadic and the result of a unique relationship in the life history of this particular person.

An antisocial criminal is in perpetual conflict with society and will engage in violent behavior as long as there is no significant change in his basic personality. On the other hand, there are relationships that are conflicted and lead to explosive behavior as the result of breakdown of the existing defenses. The intense ambivalent relationship characteristic of sadomasochistic marriage falls into this category. The masochistic husband kills his wife as the result of a breakdown of the existing structure which was responsible for the maintenance of the sadomasochistic relationship.

The antisocial criminal's behavior is due to structuralization of aggression, whereas the masochistic husband's act of murder is the result of destructuralization. Other examples of structuralized aggression are duels, warfare, and the planned crimes of professional armed robbers. The latter can be controlled at times by the victim through his behavior. For example, in an armed robbery, surrender of the valuables leads to cessation of the aggression. In a duel, acceptance of humiliation puts an end to the lethal threat. In other words, humiliation can be exchanged for annihilation. In organized warfare, surrender means the end of hostilities. In ritualized, structuralized aggression, the reality principle still prevails.

But aggression that is impulsive cannot be controlled by the victim as a rule. A disorganized mob attempting to lynch a prisoner will not be diverted from its destructive path by the waving of a white flag. Similarly, an individual in a dissociative state of mind will not be satisfied by symbolic surrender.

To understand the causes of murder more clearly, and therefore to try to bring about prevention, I have been led by my case material to separate homicidal behavior into three categories: egosyntonic homicide, egodystonic (or dissociative) homicide, and psychotic homicide.

To understand the categories, let us first consider the anatomy of personality, which can be conceptualized along the following lines. There is a basic core, the animal part of every human being, called the *id*, with which we are born. As child-rearing progresses, certain interactions occur between child and parent, and another layer of personality forms which we call the *ego*. It is the executive part of our personality; it controls our motility and our rational thinking processes and exercises some control over our impulses. The third structure is called *superego*. It roughly corresponds to what is popularly known as conscience, based on the child's identifying with the standards of behavior of his parents or other significant adults in the environment.

Some murders in our society are committed because they serve a purpose that is acceptable to the rational mind, or the ego. Take a soldier who kills an enemy. This is an act he is trained to do, feels he should do. A policeman who kills a criminal who tries to escape is also doing something acceptable to his way of thinking. Behavior which is acceptable to the ego of the individual is called "egosyntonic."

A duel may lead to murder, but it represents an example of organized, ritualized aggression. A lethal confrontation portrayed in a western movie is another organized form of behavior with definite rules of procedure, as is a gangland killing, an organized form of behavior carried out by those who believe in violence as a way of ending conflict. These models of egosyntonic slayings have dominated the way we handle homicide, even though they do not constitute the majority of murders. A variety of terms are used to describe the mental state that allows for deliberate choice: decision, resolution, intention, volition. The law is explicit about this state of mind when it uses such words and phrases as "mens rea," "intent," "maliciously and wilfully," "knowingly." The law turns to the behavioral expert for answers to the questions about the state of mind of the murderer prior to and at the time of the act. Inquiry into his state of mind has far-reaching implications not only for legal purposes but also for the prevention of homicide. It is important for the lawyer and the psychiatrist to know to what extent the individual "was himself" at the time the act was carried out.

There is another type of behavior that is not acceptable to the ego, behavior which in psychiatry is called "egodystonic." For example, a person has to wash his hands fifty times a day even though this is not rationally acceptable to him; he feels forced to do it. Similarly, there are homicides that occur against the conscious wishes of the murderer; the majority of homicides fall into this category.

What I call "egodystonic" homicide describes a killing that occurs against the conscious wishes of the perpetrator and is usually carried out in an altered state of consciousness, occurring without conscious awareness or conscious motivation.

The concept of "dissociation" is essential to the understanding of egodystonic homicidal behavior. This term was introduced by Pierre Janet (1859–1947) to describe a mental state where a part of the psychic structure is split off from the rest of the personality. Dissociation is a defense mechanism even though it involves disruption of the ego. It is analogous to fainting in physiology. In fainting, certain physiological functions are disrupted as an adaptive measure. The essence of the dissociative state is that certain functions of the personality escape from the control of the individual. Dissociation is observed in many situations, usually without serious consequences. The term "dissociation" encompasses a variety of altered states of consciousness which result from various causes, either psychological, physiological, or pharmacological.

Dr. Karl Menninger in his book *The Vital Balance* describes this state as "ego rupture," which he defines as a major disorganization of the ego which is reversible. He also introduces the term "episodic discontrol," which encompasses various situations popularly described as "going to pieces." He points out that other authors have used such terms as "situational psychosis," "ten-day schizophrenia," "shell-shock," "combat exhaustion," conditions that are results of being placed in situations of insoluble conflicts. He describes dissociation also as a means of control of aggression, saying, "Dissociative loss of consciousness is actually a device for the control of aggressions and not merely, as it is sometimes assumed, a self-anesthetizing device in states of fear."

Since the terms "situational psychosis," "ten-day schizophrenia," and other similar descriptive labels are not in the current nomenclature, I use the term "dissociative reaction," which is included in the official nomenclature of the American Psychiatric Association.

The ego may be viewed as an electrical fuse. It can take only so much emotional tension. If the tension builds up to a degree beyond the capacity of the ego to accept it, then a disruption occurs. It can be brief or long-lasting. If the latter, we speak of it as psychotic, or, in popular language, crazy or insane. If the former, we speak of a "dissociative state," a disruption of consciousness. While it lasts, a dissociative state is the functional equivalent of a psychosis. It actually occurs every night in all of us. When we fall asleep, our ego is relatively inoperative and we become psychotic. During dreams we perform acts or have thoughts that are irrational. We may dream all the murders we wish and no one will punish us. A dissociative state may also occur when a person is under extreme stress, is very tired, takes certain drugs like LSD, or drinks too much alcohol. It is no accident that many murders occur when men and women are under the influence of alcohol and their usual ego-defenses have fallen.

Thus homicide, in my view, can be classified as egosyntonic, which is acceptable to the personality, such as the killings committed by a soldier or a policeman or even the mercy killing performed by a doctor; egodystonic, which is not acceptable to the individual and which occurs when his mind is in a state of dissociation; and psychotic.

We might ask why it is that the person who commits a murder of which he does not consciously approve has entered a relationship that is so explosive it can only end in murder. The answer is that he has unconsciously sought the repetition of his childhood patterns, the ones that are familiar to him. If a child has had emotionally nourishing relationships, he will as an adult seek the kind of person who will provide similar relationships. If a child has endured emotionally destructive relationships, as an adult he will unconsciously seek the kind of person who will be destructive, or on whom he can at last wreak his long-smoldering revenge as he experiences a tension his ego can no longer control.

The superego, whose purpose is to make us "good" and acceptable to our parents and the world, may also lead us to commit one of the most horrible of crimes—murder. The superego frequently becomes the source of cruelty toward the self and others.

The nature of the superego's relation to the self and to others depends greatly on the relationship between a child and his parents. Cruel parents perpetuate their cruelty through the agency of the superego in their offspring. When I first began studying murderers, I was struck by how "good" they were prior to committing the act of murder, and afterward as well. Here were people regarded by friends and relatives as highly moral, upstanding individuals who avoided unkindness, who preached and most of the time practiced the inhibition of aggressive activities. I was struck by the fact that these individuals not only refrained from aggressive behavior but also avoided thoughts that were of aggressive nature. They were law-abiding to the extreme. It has become a half-serious, half-joking witticism of mine to say to friends, "Beware of the man who never has had a traffic ticket." Many of the murderers I have examined never had.

Murderers of the egodystonic type, the majority of murderers, show specific features which I call the "aggressophobic personality." Such persons are rigid, moralistic, and highly conflicted about their own aggressive strivings. Their aggressive feelings and impulses are repressed and come to conscious awareness only when packaged by a protective layer of rationalizations. These are the people who will tell you that they would not hurt a fly but will defend the right of a homeowner to shoot a bicycle thief, an actual case. "Aggressophobe" is my term for a person afflicted with an overdeveloped superego. His ego constantly yearns for a superego approval it can never fully achieve. The dependence of the ego on the superego is a continuation of a child's dependence on parents for approval and acceptance. The murderers of the disassociative type are individuals whose superego is demanding, cruel, and unpredictable in its approval, very much like the parents of childhood. The aggressophobe shows an inability to express aggression on all levels. Absence of aggressive fantasies is very typical for him. Frequently such individuals are even unable to understand questions about fantasies since they have to deny ever having indulged in the thought of aggression. Their repressed aggression is projected on others, and therefore paranoid preoccupations take the place of aggressive fantasies and daydreams of revenge on harsh bosses or selfish mates.

A middle-aged executive was involved in an accident caused by a drug-intoxicated teenager. He suffered physical injury from which he quickly recovered, but he continued to be afflicted by a variety of psychosomatic symptoms and anxiety attacks. In psychotherapy it came out that his major conflict was over his rage at the drug-using girl who had caused the accident. He recalled that while sharing the ambulance with her, he experienced an intense homicidal rage, a desire to kill her, which he repressed. An important clue to his personality was the design of his home, of ranch-type construction with three "safety stations," one at each end and one in the middle of the house. A safety station, he explained, was a specially designed small closet containing a telephone, fire extinguisher, and loaded gun, ready for use. Though he lived in a low-crime suburb and had never been victimized, he was preoccupied with crime; he read avidly the accounts of criminal activity in nearby Detroit and other major cities throughout the country. The reality of crime in these cities he used as displacement for his own murderous impulses.

The aggressophobe was recognized by Shakespeare in the line "Thus conscience doth make cowards of us all." The fearful preoccupation with crime and attacks from the outside is a hallmark of such individuals. The communist-hunters of yesterday are probably among the crime fighters of today. I do not mean to imply that communism is not a danger to the survival of capitalism or to minimize the reality of crime in American society. On the contrary, the reality of these dangers provides a good target for the expression of displaced aggressive emotion. The danger the aggressophobe faces is the possible failure of his effort to contain his mounting, repressed rage. He can express aggression only in explosive fashion, and he is therefore forever on the brink of losing his rigid grip and falling into the abyss of unbridled rage. Crime, communists, fascists, racists, Jews, blacks are but a few of the assorted rationalized targets that allow the aggressophobe to smuggle some quantity of aggressive contraband past the watchful superego. The aggressophobe is forever in search of a good hate object, that is, a seal of approval from the superego for the expression of aggression.

On a more personal level, the aggressophobe acquires love objects which are also good hate objects. It is rather common in the practice of psychiatry to see a passive, paranoid, masochistic man married to an aggressive, hysterical, sadistic female. Or the marriage of the Suffering Susan to the sadistic, alcoholic man who beats her and fails to provide for the family, though she loves him in spite of or because of it. This type of relationship is known in psychiatry as the sadomasochistic relationship. Such a relationship is based on the existence of an aggressive bond between two or more individuals. The sadomasochistic relationship is most frequently encountered in a dyadic group, often in marriages but not infrequently between parent and child, two business partners, or siblings. Such relationships exist also between an individual and an institution, such as church, corporation, or military, and even between persons and their pets. The aggressive behavior which occurs between individuals involved in sadomasochistic relationships provides little positive gratification of aggression, that is, aggressive fulfillment, the sense of satiation. What we observe instead is an ever-increasing, positive balance of aggression leading to increasing levels of aggressive tension. The sadomasochistic relationship is a defense against open expression of the aggressive drive and its derivatives. Aggression is gratified through a variety of defensive maneuvers like masochism, moral sadism, or imposition of sacrifices on the self and others.

Sometimes war offers the aggressophobe a chance to explode. I examined a twenty-year-old black soldier who had committed a murder while in Vietnam. One night while on base he saw a white sergeant lying on the ground in a drunken stupor. Nearby there was an ax. The black soldier picked up the ax and killed the white sergeant. He tried to rationalize his deed by "black power" rhetoric. I saw in the base dispensary records the following note, entered four months before the murder:

> This man was seen today requesting an N-P [neuropsychiatric] consult. Main problem centers about fear of someone, especially a white person, harming him at night. No problem during day. After a long examination I can find no evidence of psychosis or neurosis. He is tense and anxious but not hostile.

Three months later, he was referred for another psychiatric evaluation with the following note:

C-M Pfc., USMC, has been under treatment for chancroid by BAS and MSA. Has been very antagonistic and paranoid re race while under treatment. He has not adjusted well into command, e.g., doesn't accept orders well, antisocial, etc., since his arrival here. Appears to get along well with his peers. He is currently facing several minor charges by company which may or may not be pressed. Please evaluate.

Two days later he was evaluated by a military psychiatrist who wrote:

The patient presents vague complaints of being scared and having feelings that people are watching him. The patient apparently had a rather chaotic home life, i.e., being shipped back and forth between his father, his mother and his grandmother. The patient describes his father as a person who drinks a lot of liquor and fights and curses all the time. The patient stated that as a youngster he received a lot of whipping from his father because he (the patient) was always in some sort of trouble.

He was diagnosed as suffering from "depressive reaction," was admitted to the psychiatric ward, where he spent a few weeks, was discharged, and shortly thereafter killed the sergeant.

He told me that one of his earliest memories, at the age of six, was seeing his father shoot his mother. Another vivid memory was of his father ordering him to cut down a tree with a butcher knife and, when he was unable to carry out his task, beating him severely. The history of exposure to sadism in early childhood was clearly responsible for his paranoid illness in adulthood.

We have here evidence that four months prior to the murder he could have been viewed as having a homicidal behavioral system ready for action. The drunken white sergeant and the ax at hand symbolically served to activate his rage, the drunken sergeant perhaps reminding him of his drunken father, and the ax, a sharp blade, bringing back memories of the butcher knife and the beating he got from his father when he failed to cut down the tree.

The soldier was obviously in emotional trouble, as the earlier reports showed. No help was given, and he was unable to

control his aggression. I use the term "aggression" to refer to a
psychic force which manifests itself by specific feelings, fantasies,
and overt behavior. These manifestations are generally described
in popular language as anger, which is an emotion. This emotion
can be experienced consciously or be repressed or denied; its
existence then has to be inferred from behavior. When an individual is overwhelmed by pleasurable stimuli, we speak of ecstasy;
when the state of being overwhelmed is induced by anger, we
speak of rage.

Another concept essential to the discussion of homicide is that
of destructive capacity. This refers to the ability to inflict harm on
another person. This ability fluctuates and is dependent on
psychic and physical development. The infant has a very limited
destructive capacity, even though he frequently develops intense
rage. He lacks physical power and sufficient maturation to use
weapons, except for his teeth.

Destructive capacity is relative. A man of medium size can
usually inflict considerable harm on a child or woman but may not
be able to inflict much damage by mere physical strength on
another, larger man. An adult has considerable destructive capacity in relation to a child. Women who kill children do so frequently without the use of any of the usual weapons. I have seen
a number of cases where children were killed by being pushed
down stairs or hit over the head with a household item such as an
iron.

The destructive capacity can be sufficient to lead a person
only to inflict harm—or it can reach a lethal level. In adult situations,
this usually involves acquisition of a weapon. The significance of
destructive capacity for the incidence of murder is best illustrated
by a hypothetical comparison. Let us assume that one hundred
husbands develop a homicidal state and attack their wives with
bare hands. Two or three murders might result. If, on the other
hand, one hundred husbands attack their wives with blunt instru-
ments, six wives possibly might die. If we assume that the
hypothetical homicidal husbands are armed with knives, the death
rate might rise to ten or fifteen. But if the attacks are carried out
with a gun, it is likely that seventy murders will result. This
presupposes the absence of conscious determination to kill and
the lack of planning and preparation.

A certain level of homicide is inevitable, but it need not be forever increasing. Prevention means not total elimination but a significant reduction in incidence.

Confronted with the problem of homicide, society turns to lawyers and policemen for answers. This is based on an unfortunate misunderstanding and is similar to an effort to obtain the cure for a deadly disease by consulting the undertakers who bury the dead bodies. Handling the victims of homicide does not make one an authority on the prevention of homicide. Prevention requires, in my opinion, first the acceptance of homicide as a natural phenomenon. People will always kill people. The issue is not *whether* homicides will occur but *how many*.

The functions of criminal law are retribution, deterrence, and rehabilitation. Rehabilitation and deterrence are prominently featured in the various discussions pertaining to criminal law, but, as a practical matter, criminal law today primarily administers punishment in the hope that it will have a deterrent effect on future criminal behavior.

Punishment imposed under criminal law is justified as having preventive value. The concept of deterrence, a cherished notion of the legal system, is accepted without much empirical evidence to support it. On mere theoretical grounds, one could attribute to deterrence an effectiveness only in the reflective, egosyntonic type of criminal behavior, the minority. Certainly deterrence is of little consequence in behavior that is symptomatic of underlying emotional illness. Crime which is motivated in large part by the need for punishment, which applies to the majority of murderers, will not be prevented by the imposition of criminal sanctions.

There are important differences in the taking of preventive measures and the imposition of criminal sanctions. Criminal sanction is retrospective. Preventive measures are directed toward the future. The very essence of punishment is the imposition of conditions designed to produce suffering. Preventive measures and medical treatment might involve suffering, but not as an essential component. There is no doubt that punishment plays a large role in the development of "normal" individuals. There are, however, those on whom punishment has no preventive effect, such as the "in cold blood" killers and those who have committed a murder for unconscious reasons.

There is a defense of insanity in the law due to the simple fact that some crimes are committed as a result of "insanity"; or, to express it psychiatrically, there are some crimes that are symptoms of a mental disorder. In 1868 the Michigan Supreme Court recognized this as an essence of the insanity defense (*People v. Garbutt*, 17 Mich. 9, 1868), when they defined insanity as a situation in which the disorder is "the efficient cause of the crime."

The defense of insanity has a variety of useful functions, which appear to have been lost in the hue and cry about coddling criminals. The defense of insanity is essential for the internal coherence of the legal structure. If criminal sanctions are based on criminal responsibility, then involuntary behavior has to be excluded from the criminal process. The defense of insanity fulfills an important social function by protecting sick people from punishment and further aggravation of their condition. Punishment of those who have transgressed provisions of the criminal law without the ability to control their behavior is offensive to the sense of justice and therefore undermines respect for the law. Such punishment has no justification regardless of the basic objectives of criminal law, whether they be those of retribution, deterrence, or rehabilitation. The defense of insanity also has some fiscal significance, since it reduces the burden that we place on our penal system of having to care for people who do not require the complex and expensive services of our penal institutions.

The defense of insanity also opens the door for psychiatry in the courtroom, which is certainly beneficial to the law, and possibly useful to psychiatry. Psychiatry has a humanizing influence on criminal law. The best example of this is the handling of suicide. Through the use of the insanity defense, suicide has been transformed from a felony to a medical entity, exciting little interest in the criminal law. Society does not appear to have suffered as a result of this evolution, and certainly the individual citizens afflicted by suicidal impulses are better served by psychiatry, inadequate as it is, than by the criminal process. It is my conviction that the insanity defense, which at the present time is rarely used, poorly presented, and frequently unsuccessful, will nevertheless succeed in transforming our irrational handling of homicide offenders into a realistic and useful system of disposition.

In handling homicides, the law uses the model of the criminal who willfully and maliciously kills another human being for some utilitarian purpose. This model fits certain homicide offenders; however, as I have pointed out, the majority of murderers do not fit this particular concept. They can be considered within this structure only by doing violence to basic legal principles, to the sense of justice, and last but not least, to the findings of behavioral science. The law as a rational system cannot survive if it continues to disregard, in principle or in practice, scientific reality. In addition to the model of the criminal man, the law has also utilized the model of the sick man who is excluded from criminal sanction. This concept has been leading a shadowy existence and is treated as a stepchild of psychiatry and the law. The insanity defense is quite prominent in the law library but disreputable in the courtroom. The indiscriminate charge of first degree murder, utilized by the prosecution in most homicides, raises no legal eyebrows. The assertion of the insanity defense, however, renders the legal or psychiatric practitioner suspect of intellectual dishonesty.

The adversary system is interpreted by the prosecution as requiring that rational motives be offered for the most irrational homicide. This task of the prosecution is enhanced by the almost universal need to see homicidal behavior as rational. The idea of acting without control, of not being in possession of one's faculties, is a terrifying one and is rejected not only by the jury but frequently by the perpetrator himself. Many a man would rather hang than accept the proposition that he acted without reason.

There is a common myth to the effect that crafty defense attorneys with the cooperation of unscrupulous psychiatrists bring about acquittals of murderers. The facts are that the very opposite holds true. The majority of the attorneys handling homicide cases are unskilled in the preparation and presentation of the insanity defense. This comes from sheer inexperience, since there are only a handful of attorneys who have prepared such a defense repeatedly. There may be many unscrupulous psychiatrists, but very few psychiatrists of any kind are willing or able to participate in the legal process.

Lawyers hold on to the cherished notion that social scientists in general, and psychiatrists in particular, are eager to invade the province of criminal law and attempt to reform it, pervert it, redesign it, and otherwise gain control of this legal institution. In reality, few social scientists, and almost no psychiatrists, have professional concern in the criminal law process. Neither psychiatric research nor psychiatric literature devotes any space to criminal law. In fact, one can hardly beg, borrow, or steal psychiatric interest in criminal proceedings. Crime has been neglected not only by social science but by the law itself. With the exception of a few criminal lawyers, unless the lawyer is a judge, you can hardly interest him in the criminal law. These specialists, incidentally, are as a rule held in low esteem by the legal profession. It is therefore not surprising that the insanity defense is infrequently raised and rarely results in success. Since between sixty and eighty percent of all homicide involves impulsive violence toward someone with whom the murderer has an intense relationship, most of these murderers qualify for the insanity defense. But only two percent of the cases charged with homicide have led to acquittal by reason of insanity.

Because of their strict consciences, most murderers who have impulsively committed a crime give themselves up. In the more than one hundred homicides I have examined, there were only a few where even halfhearted attempts were made to elude apprehension. In most instances, the murderer called the police or reported to the police station. It hardly requires the skills of Sherlock Holmes or the resources of Scotland Yard to apprehend this particular category of homicide offenders. Futhermore, it does not require brilliant advocacy to persuade a jury that the murderer did know what he was doing and that therefore it is the duty of the jury to find him guilty of first degree murder. For some reason beyond my comprehension, prosecutors in this country consider it their duty to obtain a first degree conviction as often as possible. The young man in the case in this book who killed his mother suddenly, then tried to have sexual relations with her, was charged with first degree murder, as though this were a sane act.

The insanity defense could be viewed, as a practical matter, to be not a defense at all but a form of guilty plea. In asserting the defense of insanity, the perpetrator admits the act and submits himself to a disposition prescribed by the law subsequent to his so-called acquittal. In other words, acquittal by virtue of insanity involves the confession of the act and the acceptance of a legally prescribed disposition that could be called a sentence. Successful assertion of the defense of insanity does not bring freedom with it. Not guilty by virtue of insanity, operationally speaking, means the acceptance of an indeterminate sentence. Therefore the defense of insanity leads primarily to a moral vindication. The control over the perpetrator is retained by the state subsequent to the acquittal by reason of insanity. How the state chooses to exercise this control will vary. In any other acquittal, the state relinquishes control over the defendant.

The majority of murderers, generally decent, law-abiding people prior to their acts, continue to be decent and law-abiding after they have killed, and practically never commit the same or any other crime. It is barbaric, I believe, to incarcerate in prison for long terms or life emotionally troubled men and women who, in a moment of insane fury, commit a crime they are not likely to repeat. The plea of insanity as a defense should be recognized as valid in such cases. The troubled person can be committed to a mental hospital instead of prison, where he may receive psychiatric help.

I believe that if we truly want to lower the rate of homicide, the need for gun control is imperative. The easy availability of weapons in general, and firearms in particular, is a significant factor in the high incidence of homicide. If murder were committed primarily by people determined to kill, it would not matter whether we had gun control legislation, but most murders are committed impulsively.

The approach to homicide in the United States has been dominated by the "rotten apple" theory, a natural by-product of our entrusting homicide prevention exclusively to lawyers and law enforcement officials. The proponents of the "rotten apple" approach say, "Take the guns out of the hands of the criminal elements, the sick, and the narcotics addicts, and we will drastically reduce the homicide rate." But it seems that no one wants to take the time to discover whether the criminal element, the sick, and the narcotics addicts really are responsible for the majority of homicides, though the information is readily available. We avoid this information because the fact that murderous wishes are universal is as repugnant as it is real. Research shows that promiscuous ownership of guns is the major factor responsible for

25,000 deaths and 200,000 injuries annually. Since 1930 Gallup polls have repeatedly shown that the majority of citizens of this country favor some type of gun-control legislation. But no political action has followed. The emotional need to ignore the data on homicide is powerful and appears immune to logic.

Up to 1967 the homicide rate in Detroit never exceeded one hundred a year. At that point, the ownership of guns tripled, owing to the riots of that year and the fear that followed. Within five years the homicide rate increased sevenfold. In 1971 the total number of homicides in Detroit was 690; handguns were responsible for 426, long guns for 133, knives for 72, other weapons for 59. The nonfirearm homicides had not markedly increased. In 1974 Detroit had a homicide rate of 54 per 100,000 population, whereas its sister city, Windsor, Ontario, separated by a narrow body of water, had 4 homicides per 100,000.

Homicide is a major public-health problem. Comparative studies of the homicide rates in other countries show it to be preventable. The recognition of certain items as dangerous to health or damaging to property usually leads to individual avoidance and government control. The mere suggestion that cyclamates might be carcinogenic brought about their virtual disappearance from the market. Studded tires were an asset to drivers during winter, but after it was determined that they were damaging to roads they were legislated out of existence with very little controversy. However, an entirely arbitrary rule without public support or, at least, acquiescence is difficult to enforce. A combination of education and legislation is therefore essential for the success of an epidemiological approach to homicide control in the United States. We must remember that epidemics were never controlled by individual good will and high-minded compliance with sanitary measures; they had to be enforced by public-health legislation.

Guns are bought ostensibly to hunt animals, to protect the home, and by authorities to enforce the law. But they are used most frequently to kill wives, husbands, lovers, children, and parents. The mere possession of a gun places the owner in danger of becoming a murderer. The damage resulting from homicide involves many more victims than the slain person. The murderer, regardless of the outcome of the legal proceedings, is irreparably damaged by his act. The relatives of both victim and perpetrator suffer great loss. Even witnesses to homicide may suffer long-term emotional difficulties.

"When guns are outlawed, only outlaws will have guns" is a slogan used by opponents of gun-control legislation. This is an accurate, though incomplete, statement. When guns are outlawed, only the outlaws and the police will have guns. And that is as it should be. The outlaws and the police need the guns in pursuit of their respective occupational goals.

The present easy availability and inexpensiveness of guns amount to a societal subsidy of the tools of crime. The professional photographer is a beneficiary of the popularity of photography. The mass consumption of photographic film insures easy availability and inexpensiveness of photographic materials. Similarly, the popularity of guns assures the professional criminal of an easy and inexpensive supply of the tools of his trade. When guns are outlawed, the police will have an advantage over the criminal. The police will be able to get guns more easily than the criminal, whereas at the present time the reverse is true. Morphine and other narcotics have been outlawed, and only doctors and outlaws can obtain them. Free availability of narcotics would inevitably increase the number of addicts in our society. There are obviously many factors that account for drug addiction, but the drug is the most easily manipulable variable in this complex phenomenon.

The first step in dealing with an illness is to study its relationship to the environment. Disease, like health, requires an appropriate environment to thrive. The history of tuberculosis, syphilis, and the plague is a history not only of pathogenic microorganisms but also of illness-enhancing environments. To illustrate this point in relation to homicide, let us assume that we are given the assignment of promoting murder. What kind of plan could we devise?

Our first step would be to make available an effective yet inexpensive tool of murder which could be easily concealed and immediately effective, so that there would be no time for thought to interfere with the impulse to kill. It is doubtful that any modern engineering firm, given this assignment, could improve on the handgun.

Our next task would be to convince a great many people that they should acquire this instrument of death. After all, people are generally squeamish about the acquisition of dangerous objects. One would have to conduct a major propaganda campaign to convince people that ownership of this item was not dangerous, indeed was highly desirable. We could even create a myth that this implement had protective value. Through appropriate influence, we might persuade the entertainment industry to feature this product in movies and television productions. Our goal would be to elevate our deadly gadget to a symbol of masculinity, courage, and virtue.

Our grand design to increase the homicide rate would be a failure if we merely induced people to acquire deadly weapons. We would also have to create conditions and situations of insoluble conflict between individuals. How do you produce conflict which is difficult to resolve? Put together angry, frustrated people, and convince them that to express anger is evil and to be avoided at all cost. Make the resolution of such conflict-ridden unions insoluble in principle and difficult as a practical matter. Successful breeding of such relationships, known as sadomasochistic, combined with widespread ownership of handguns, is the formula for fulfillment of our hypothetical goal of promotion of homicide.

It so happens that we do have an effective and cheap murder weapon, namely, the handgun. We also have a mystique surrounding this item, and we have many forces that promote sadomasochistic relationships. In short, institutionalized homicide is part of our societal structure.

Murder and photography have a great deal in common. Widespread amateur interest in photography assures easy availability of inexpensive cameras and film to the professionals. Similarly, the widespread interest in and use of firearms assures easy availability of guns and ammunition to the professionals. The analogy between murder and photography breaks down, however, when it comes to promotion and advertising. Whereas Kodak and other photographic manufacturers must depend on their own financial and creative resources to advertise their products, the manufacturers of guns need not concern themselves with such activities. The advertising and promotion of guns is carried out by movies, television, fiction writers, and toy manufacturers. This form of promotion is much more effective than conventional advertising and has the additional advantage of being free. The government also participates in this blatant discrimination in its practice of distributing, at no charge, surplus firearms to gun clubs; it certainly must have surplus cameras and film as well. Many states have passed laws which provide for inspection of guns by technically trained personnel, free of charge. Why not establish a similar network of camera inspectors who would check the proper functioning of photographic equipment? Equal benefits under the law should be provided to citizens regardless of what they are shooting—cameras or guns. The two activities deserve equal governmental attention, since they are both family-oriented. Research shows that both camera owners and gun owners prefer, as subjects of their shooting, members of their family and close acquaintances with whom they have intense emotional relationships.

Another slogan used by the opponents of gun control is "Guns don't kill people; people kill people." This statement is certainly true and gives us the option of eliminating people or guns. To change people into creatures incapable of aggressive impulses would be like trying to cure prostitution by eliminating the sexual drive. The cure would be worse than the disease. There will never be a time when homicide will significantly decrease if the number of firearms remains high.

Given a certain number of firearms in circulation, a predictable number of firearm-related accidents, suicides, and homicides will result. The most reliable guideline for estimating the number of firearms in circulation is the number of firearm accidents that occur in a given community.

The traditional legal measures of registration, licensing, and inspection have no bearing on the reduction of firearm-related deaths unless they appreciably reduce the number of firearms in circulation. From the standpoint of homicide prevention, it is meaningless whether the gun is registered, licensed, or inspected. The mere presence of the weapon, regardless of its legal status, creates a statistical probability for the occurrence of murder.

Since the majority of homicides involve people who have a close relationship, it is not surprising that killer and victim are usually of the same racial origin. American society is still racially segregated when it comes to intimate relationships. The incidence of intermarriage and sexual involvement between blacks and whites remains relatively low; close business partnerships between blacks and whites are also infrequent. In the absence of intimate relationships between blacks and whites, the explosive discharges of aggression also remain segregated. Explosive discharges of aggression are, however, more common among blacks, which is not surprising in view of the oppression to which black citizens have been subjected. Oppression leads to suppressed anger, a precondition for the occurrence of explosive discharge of aggression. The adjusted homicide rate in the black population is significantly higher than that among whites. Eighty percent of the 1974 victims of homicide in Detroit were black. Kurt Gorwitz, director of research and analysis for the Office of Health and Medical Affairs of the State of Michigan, pointed out in a recent study that between 1961 and 1971 the death rate from homicides among young black men increased more than 230 percent. By 1971, accidents and murder were responsible for half of all deaths among black men ages fifteen to forty-four. Homicide prevention should therefore be an issue of vital interest to responsible leaders of the black community. In the racially polarized society of the United States, black and white political leaders have exploited the fears of their constituents by opposing gun-control legislation. Certain white politicians, under the euphemism of law and order, have for a long time played on the fears of the white community to promote their political goals. More recently, certain black politicians have followed the same approach. It is a moral obligation of all political leaders to inform their constituents of the well-established fact that gun ownership offers very little protection and leads to the loss of a great many lives and to innumerable tragedies.

Why do people want to own guns? Why are they so jealous of their right to "bear arms"? Why is the controversy about guns so intense, and why is it frequently dominated by irrational arguments?

My clinical contact with gun owners indicates that guns offer a sense of security and protection. The gun owner feels safe and secure with a gun at his side, though he is guided by emotional and not realistic considerations. He feels secure because of the proximity of the gun, and this has to be accepted as a psychological fact. The characterization of gun-control laws as "taking away" guns, a phrase used frequently by the opponents of such legislation, symbolizes the gun as a bodily appendage, so that giving up the gun in fantasy is submitting to mutilation. The overvaluation of the gun by its owner clearly identifies the gun as a libidinal object. Most dedicated owners handle their guns with obvious pleasure, cleaning and polishing them almost reverently. The narcissistic investment in the gun as an extension of the self is often very apparent. The equation of gun with penis is attested to in such expressions as "to shoot off your gun," referring to ejaculation. In the Marine Corps it was forbidden to use the term "gun" for rifle, and those who transgressed this unofficial code were punished by noncommissioned officers by being required to go from one barracks to another holding in one hand their rifle and in the other their penis, announcing, "This is a rifle and this is a gun. This is for shooting and this is for fun." In the symbolic language of dreams, the gun often stands for the penis.

The gun owner generally says he has a gun because of the fear of crime. What crime? Attacks by strangers on himself or on those he loves, he will respond. Since these dangers are universal, the question as to why some men acquire guns and others do not remains unanswered. Gun ownership and dedication to the gun preceded the recent staggering increase in the crime rate.

The dangers associated with crime are not only physical but psychic. The ownership of a gun alters the psychic reality of the owner by making him immune to the danger of ever having to choose between flight and submission. He feels, "I can stand my own ground." He need not be a coward and submit in humiliation.

A young man who was rather short shot and killed a girl friend. When asked why he owned a gun, he said he had bought it for his girl's protection. When asked the same question under sodium amytal, he responded, "Man, with a gun I feel ten feet tall!" Jack Ruby, when I interviewed him at the request of his family, told me he always carried a gun, then added the qualification, "Except when I go into a synagogue." I asked, "Why not in a synagogue?" All he would say is, "You just don't." It seemed that in a synagogue he felt secure and did not need a gun. Passivity and insecurity are the major characterological features leading to the need for a gun. On a narcissistic level, the acquisition of a gun often serves to enhance or repair a lowered self-image. Sadistic fantasies are frequently in the foreground, based on the wish to inflict pain and suffering on real or imagined enemies. On a conscious level, there are altruistic and realistic reasons for the acquisition of firearms for the purpose of protection of the self and others from external dangers.

The unwritten law of American political life in relation to gun control has been never to attack the gun as such. Only the irresponsible gun owner, generally portrayed as a criminal or a mentally ill person, is mentioned as the possible object of governmental interest. This immunity of the gun from criticism is another indication that it is a libidinal object. Mothers and guns are attacked at great peril to one's political and even personal future. I have been repeatedly threatened for my gun-control advocacy.

The gun lobby and gun owners delight in criticizing people who misuse guns, who, according to them, fall into three categories: persons who lack know-how in the use of this valued object; those who do not deserve the privilege to bear arms, namely, criminals; and people who by virtue of sickness cannot be entrusted with gun ownership.

The greatest scorn is reserved for those who don't know how to use weapons and don't know how to take care of them. The need for "training" in the use of firearms is repeatedly emphasized in gun circles and contributes to the gun mystique. The simple fact is that according to FBI statistics, the overwhelming majority of murderers have had no training in the use of firearms and, in fact, fired their first shot when they killed someone.

It is apparent that little training, if any, is needed to effectively use a gun in civilian life. The argument that lack of training accounts for homicide is frequently advanced, but it has no logical or empirical merit. It does, however, make sense as an expression of scorn for lack of libidinal investment in an overvalued object. A man who does not know "how to use it" is an object of disrespect in gun circles. One frequently hears the derogatory comment, "He doesn't know his way around with guns." It requires little perceptiveness to recognize the analogy to impotence and lack of virility.

I testified once in the trial of a man who saved his wife from committing suicide with a gun. He wrestled it from her, then sat exhausted, holding the deadly weapon. She lurched for it. The gun, which had a hair trigger, discharged, and she lay dead. The man was charged with first degree murder. I testified on his behalf. The prosecutor tried to discredit me by showing the jury I knew nothing about guns. He also requested I pull the trigger to see how much pressure was required. I expressed reluctance to touch the pistol and protested it was irrelevant to my psychiatric opinion. But the judge ordered me to carry out the prosecutor's request. To the delight of the prosecutor, I pulled the trigger with obvious distaste. The predominantly female jury returned a verdict of "not guilty." My credibility and competency as a psychiatrist were not discredited by my lack of competence with and distaste for guns. Perhaps a predominantly male jury would have been impressed by the prosecutor's stratagem.

If protection from attack were the main basis for the acquisition of guns, one would expect women to show great interest in guns. The same would apply to old and weak men. In fact, however, the greatest interest in guns is found among young and middle-aged men in the prime of life and at the height of their castration anxiety.

To justify their opposition to gun control, gun owners and their lobby emphasize three major points: that they have the right to own guns (the constitutional right to bear arms); that there is injustice in having guns taken away (the confiscation issue); and that there are always those who wish to have guns illegally ("When guns are outlawed, only outlaws will have guns").

These three arguments have little rational validity. The Constitution does not mention individual ownership of guns. There have been no proposals to take guns away from owners without compensation. And clearly, the argument that only criminal elements will have guns is not very impressive since policemen will have guns also. No one advances the view that heroin and morphine should be sold in supermarkets because narcotics addicts can obtain them on the black market. These three arguments are comprehensible only when viewed in terms of the underlying castration anxiety engendered by the thought of being "deprived" of a gun.

The gun is a substitute object which is effective in controlling the level of castration anxiety in men who feel threatened. The threat of the loss of the gun heightens their anxiety and leads at times to irrational responses. Gun ownership is what psychiatrists call a behavioral expression of reaction-formation to an underlying fear of passivity. The annual ritual known as the hunting season, in which thousands of men go into the woods with guns and alcohol, is an institutionalized form of this behavior. Hundreds of men die in the performance of this ritual.

If we want to prevent many unnecessary murders, the most easily manipulable variable in the homicidal process is the availability of the weapon. Statistical evidence and clinical studies indicate a positive correlation between the incidence of murder and the availability of guns. The National Commission on the Causes and Prevention of Violence, using data provided by the Chicago Police Department, concluded that the fatality rate of firearm attacks is about five times higher than the fatality rate of attacks with knives. Since 1900, more than 800,000 Americans have been killed with privately owned guns.

I echo a request made originally by Camus: "All I ask is that, in the midst of a murderous world, we agree to reflect on murder and to make a choice."

The pathology of aggression has never been fully described in a manner analogous to the description of the pathology of the libido. There is much more literature on the state of "being in love" as a bond between individuals than about the state of "being in hate." The vicissitudes of the libidinal drive are much more extensively described and understood than the vicissitudes of the aggressive drive, particularly in regard to its bond-forming quality.

I believe most murderers are afflicted with an "over-developed" superego. They have never been able to develop a pattern of aggressive gratification on a physical or verbal level. To a certain degree, traditional middle-class values prohibit such gratification. When these values are imposed by violent child-rearing practices, the superego becomes a cruel and punitive master, intolerant of any overt expressions of aggression, until one day, tortured beyond its ability to bear any more repression, the mind allows the unconscious impulse to break through.

We are all capable of murder, but the person who actually commits murder is likely to have been subjected to more cruelty early in life, either physical or psychological or both, than most other children. In addition, he has felt the need to cover up, to deny his own anger at the hurt.

The murderer has usually been able to repress his wrath at whatever life offers. But suddenly a situation will arise, one he has unconsciously sought out, that approximates the one which, as a child, he thought excessively harsh and cruel. He becomes, at last, unable to repress his anger. The psychic lid flies off the Pandora's box of his impulses, and he kills—not the original targets of his wrath, but a later reasonable facsimile thereof.

It is no surprise that the majority of murderers have lived quiet lives; they are often described by family, friends, and neighbors as kindly, easygoing, polite, and considerate. Finally, though, a set of circumstances sparks this surface calm to a pitch of rage as, with knife or gun or pillow or rope or bare hands, they murder someone supposedly near and dear. Most murders are committed by overcontrolled, rigid people who are the last persons one would expect to turn out to be killers.

We might say that every murderer is a product of a sadistic parent. The sadism may be either subtle or open. There is the parent who beats or batters the child, which harms the child both physically and psychologically, for a physical injury is also psychically searing. But the vast majority of child abuses are far more disguised. They involve not an overt physical crippling by a psychotic parent who throws a child out of a window, but a slow, insidious psychological crippling that continues over a number of years. The crippling results from an excessive overprotectiveness which shows itself in a refusal to allow a child to mature psychically, to express freely his emotions of hate and love, at the same time forcing him to control them. In effect, such a parent says to the child, "You belong to me. I don't care what you are feeling. Or thinking. *My* needs come first."

It is as cruel as a beating for a parent to treat a child as chattel in a psychological sense, refusing to allow the child to experience a sense of independence, to separate emotionally. This thwarts the child's natural psychosexual growth, if not completely stifling his aggressive and sexual impulses. It is probably no accident that society has grown from one in which men enslaved other, supposedly "inferior" men, as parents do children, to one in which slavery is frowned on, as mankind slowly and painfully has grown toward a greater maturity, both emotional and intellectual.

There are few human relations that involve violence to the degree encountered within a family. Not only do parents strike, slap, and beat children, occasionally killing them, but children strike parents more often than prevailing myths allow us to recognize, sometimes killing them. Lizzie Borden lives on in our fantasy because she acted out a desire that is inevitably felt whenever childhood conflicts run deep.

Corporal punishment is the obvious, though not the exclusive, form of cruelty toward children, and in any discussion of prevention of murder, we should start with the subject of how to decrease the incidence of physical cruelty to children, the most blatant attack on a child, one that may result in his death. Such an approach is the most practical in a day when as yet there is little popular understanding of the results of psychic cruelty and not nearly enough therapists to treat emotionally disturbed parents and children. At the same time we should keep trying to promote an understanding of how parents who are unconsciously cruel to a child can foster murder in the heart of that child, who then, as an adult, will become a killer because he has suffered what I call "catastrophic conflict." Society has failed dismally to protect children from sadistic parents who cripple them emotionally; indeed, virtually all religions and cultures have considered a child's relationship to his parents to be sacred. Various measures have been adopted over the centuries to reinforce parental authority and ensure the inviolability of parents.

Parental control in early childhood, when a child is most vulnerable, is based on concrete factors like superior physical power and control of vital resources. During adolescence, this control relies increasingly on psychic forces. Adolescence, in this context, could be defined as that period during which the child has accepted control by parents even though he does not have to. It is a developmental stage leading to the ultimate shift in the means of parental control. When excessive disturbances occur during this transition, a child may kill a sadistic parent out of recognition that the act represents his only means of surviving.

As Milton wrote, "Childhood shows the man as morning shows the day." Unfortunately, there are many unwanted children, and they not only are wretched themselves but create stress within a family, making a marriage that might otherwise have survived unbearable. The unwanted child knows he is unwanted and cannot but be filled with hostile feelings toward his mother and father. The opposition to divorce, which luckily is diminishing, has perpetuated many marriages that have had a devastating psychic effect on children.

There is an urgent need for increased understanding of the disturbed family as well as for resources for effective intervention and remedial actions. Freedom in a democratic society is perfectly compatible with measures designed to control pathological behavior on the part of parents and children. Abusive behavior toward children has for too long been traditional in the Western world, with considerable ideological support from religion, law, and folklore.

Early in my work I was impressed with the accounts given by patients of the cruelty they suffered at the hands of parents. Physical beatings were commonplace; parents frequently behaved more as torturers than protective figures. In the summer of 1975 I was walking down the boat dock in Grosse Pointe, a fashionable suburb of Detroit, when I noticed a husky young man pick up a youngster who looked about five years old and throw him over a fence. The youngster fell on his back, then started to cry, obviously hurt and frightened. Dr. Douglas Sargent, a psychiatrist and a courageous, aggressive man, was with me, and we both ran up to the young man. Doug asked, "Why did you do that? You could have hurt the boy badly." The surly response was, "What's it to you? I'm the child's father." Another young man, standing nearby with his two children, echoed this sentiment, saying to us, "I don't understand what business this is of yours—he's the boy's father." Doug, never at a loss for words, said he had a right to express his indignation "because I am a citizen."

Parental cruelty causes in the mind of the growing child the development of a cruel superego (conscience) which prevents expression of aggression, leading to the child punishing himself severely not only for deeds but for thoughts and wishes of aggression. This need for punishment explains the sadomasochistic relationships many people form as they psychically torture others and are in turn psychically tortured. The inability to express aggression on a "pay-as-you-go" basis leads to a state of aggressive overload which, in turn, leads to explosive, uncontrolled discharges of aggression.

As adults, we forget how very frightening and threatening the world in which a child lives can be. Every child is extremely vulnerable to whatever stirs in the atmosphere around him. Every emotion to a child is felt as intense and dramatic. When he is angry, he is possessed by rage. When he feels deserted by his mother, he acts as though he is losing his very life. If he is physically assaulted, each blow to him is like a taste of death.

Thus the adult who is driven to murder has had, as a child, a far more brutal environment, either physically or psychologically or both, than most people. He has grown up with a consuming inner rage. He has strong fantasies of being unloved, rejected. He feels worthless, hardly a man (or, if female, a woman).

I shall proceed to discuss four cases, four men who committed murder, all of whom I interviewed and evaluated as to their sanity (their names have been changed in all cases). In three of the cases, it is obvious that each one killed a person he supposedly loved. The exception is the man who killed utter strangers, which proves not an exception if we can understand that unconsciously he murdered a man and his pregnant wife who symbolically stood for the loved/hated father and mother of his childhood.

In each instance I have tried to demonstrate that childhood held the roots of the murder. Since I did not treat these men as patients, the best I could do was to try to elicit from them as much material about their childhood as was possible in the brief time I saw them. Had I been able to study in depth the background of one murderer over a period of months or years, I might have been able to prove my point far more convincingly. But from what I obtained I can only surmise what their childhoods must have been like, as, subject to the powerful passions which occasionally possess all of us, they grew up with mothers and fathers who both consciously and unconsciously aroused their rage to an intolerable degree.

There are many things in a child's life that will make him furious, and at a very early age. Watch a child eighteen or nineteen months old and see how he acts. He feels he owns his mother and resents any intruder, such as a father or brother or sister, coming between them. He needs her to make him feel loved and secure. If she leaves him alone for one moment, he cries as though his heart will break, or screams with an anger that is pure fury. If he sees his father kiss his mother, he tries to break up this expression of love that excludes him. As he grows older, he learns to deal with frustration. If he has a wise, understanding, loving mother and father, the learning process is fairly comfortable. But if he has selfish, harsh parents, the learning process is so painful he may never learn to accept frustration or to control his anger.

In each of the following cases, though there is not enough proof to show clearly how disturbed the murderer's childhood was, there is the fact that, as an adult, he had to commit murder. That fact alone permits us to deduce some of the psychic roots of murder. No one is driven to murder unless as a child he has felt excessively murderous toward his mother and father. The very act of murder tells of a childhood that inevitably, with the slow force of a gathering tornado, leads to a fury that can no longer be held back. Though the hand of the adult holds the gun, it is the mind of the child that pulls the trigger.

2

The Nightmare

It was an April afternoon, and signs of spring were just starting to emerge along the Michigan countryside. Rolling hills were losing the barren brown of winter, softening into a readiness for bloom.

Ray Boxer, a slender man of thirty-six, with an esthetic face, blond hair, and brown eyes, was driving his white Ford along a deserted dirt road. He was looking for a job. He had been visiting friends in that area for the past three weeks.

Suddenly the engine of his car stopped, as it did every so often. He didn't know what was wrong with it; he was an artist, not a mechanic. But if he allowed the engine to rest for a while, it would always start again. He thought it might have overheated and needed time to cool off.

It was a lonely road with no traffic. He stepped out of the car to look around. Just to the rear, and about five hundred yards to the right, he saw a small white farmhouse. It appeared inviting.

A pickup truck was winding down the road toward him. It drew alongside and stopped.

An elderly man called out in a kindly voice, "Anything wrong?"

"I think my car's overheated," he said. "I'm waiting for it to cool off."

The man stepped out of his truck, holding a plastic jar. He walked over to Ray.

"Put this water in your radiator," he said. "It might help."

"Thanks." Ray unscrewed the radiator cap and poured water into the opening. He handed the jar back to the man. "Much obliged," he said.

"Not at all."

The man had a face furrowed with lines burned in by years of farming in the sun. Noticing the Missouri license plates on the white Ford, the man said, "You're a long ways from home."

"Yeah, I'm visiting friends," said Ray.

"Well, glad I could help." The farmer waved goodbye and was off.

Ray did not try to start up his car. His eyes were riveted on the farmhouse. It seemed deserted, like the dirt road in front of it. There was no sign of life, no car in the yard. He needed money. He thought he might be able to find a few dollars in the house. He started to walk toward it.

He tried the front door. It was locked. Feeling excitement stir in his stomach, as he always did when he broke into an empty house, he walked to the back door. He tried the knob. The door swung open.

He entered the kitchen. There could be nothing there of value, he thought, and walked into the living room. He looked around at plush furniture and at paintings of flowers on the walls. He saw a suitcase standing near the front door, as though someone had packed and was planning a journey.

At that moment he heard a car drive up to the house. He looked out the window. A light blue Chevrolet was parking outside the front door. There was no chance to escape now. He felt a slight fury flood his body, anger at being caught doing something forbidden.

He backed away from the window and ran to a small bedroom in the rear of the house. He noticed a shotgun hanging on the wall and a closet with a curtain hung across the doorway. He hid behind the curtain.

He waited there for about five minutes, listening to the

distant hum of voices, feeling more and more keyed up. Then he stepped out of the closet. He took the shotgun off the wall. His mind was racing. He felt guilty at being trapped in the house he had entered illegally, but he also felt excited at the power he now possessed because of the gun.

He walked into the living room. It was empty. The voices were coming from the kitchen, and he walked in there, holding the gun tight.

He confronted the startled faces of a young farmer in blue jeans, his very pregnant wife in dark blue corduroy pants, and a little girl about five years old wearing a white dress. There was fear in the eyes of the woman, who was filling a coffeepot with water from the sink. The man also looked frightened but seemed to be trying to control his fear. The little girl seemed amazed, as though he were a man from Mars.

No one said a word. Then he said, "All of you go into the living room. I won't hurt you if you'll obey." He tried to keep his voice cool.

The woman put down the coffeepot. They followed him into the living room, where he said, "Sit down."

The woman sat on the plush couch with the little girl, who held her hand tightly. The farmer sat in a large plush chair to the right of the couch. Ray sat, pointing the gun at them, on another chair covered in a flowery print.

"What can we do for you?" asked the farmer in a quiet voice.

"I don't know," Ray said. He really didn't. He had never been in this situation before, though there was something about the farmhouse that evoked memories of earlier times when he had felt very confused, not at all in a position of power, as he was now.

The little girl spoke for the first time. She said to her mother, "Can I watch television?"

The mother looked pleadingly at Ray. "May I turn on the set?" she asked. It stood in a corner of the room.

"Okay," he said.

She stood up, walked to the portable television set, and turned it on very low.

Ray said to her, "Go ahead and finish making the coffee. We can all have a cup."

"Is it all right to leave the room?" She looked at her husband worriedly.

"Go ahead, dear," he said.

He took out a pack of cigarettes and offered one to Ray. "Will you have one?"

"Thanks." Ray carefully selected a cigarette and lit it with one of his own matches.

He tried to figure out what to do. These people could have him arrested and sent to prison. They could put the finger on him for burglary. He sat in silence, as did the farmer. The little girl was watching a cartoon on television. The only sound in the room was the cackling conversation of the crazy animal characters.

The woman came in with a pot of coffee, three cups and saucers, and cream and sugar. Ray put two heaping teaspoons of sugar and a lot of cream into his cup. As he drank the coffee he felt his mind stir into action, revived.

He made small talk with the farmer and his wife. He told them he was looking for a job. He asked about the farm, said he had once lived and worked on a farm in California. They seemed interested in him, as though they would like to help him get work.

Then the woman asked if she could fix a sandwich for her little girl for supper. He told her to go ahead and make them all sandwiches. They ate the sandwiches, drank more coffee. By now it was dark outside; he guessed it was about seven o'clock.

He had made up his mind what to do. He said to them, "I have to tie you up. It will give me time to get away."

The man and woman looked at each other as though they wanted to protest, but said nothing. He assured them, "Just so you won't tell anyone about me until I'm far from here."

He said to the farmer, "I'm going to tie you up in the bedroom."

He walked over to the little girl, turned off the television set and said, "Come with your father and me." He had noticed a small bed in the back room, and he would put her into it. She still said not a word to him.

In the bedroom he said to the farmer, "Take off your boots and take the laces out of them." The rawhide laces would be useful as ropes.

The farmer took off his boots and removed the laces. Ray told him, "Lie down on your back on the bed."

He took the long laces and cut them in half with a pair of scissors lying on the bureau. He tied the farmer's right hand to one of the head bedposts, his left hand to the other. Then he tied the farmer's right foot to one of the bottom bedposts, his left foot to the other. The farmer lay spread-eagled.

He went back to the woman in the living room. He wondered what to use to tie her hands.

He said, "Take off the corduroy pants."

She looked frightened to death, as though he were going to rape her. "None of that," he said coolly. "I just want to use your pantyhose to tie you with. Take them off too."

She looked as though she were about to cry but she did as he requested, standing there with her stomach bulging out in pregnancy.

He said, "Lie down on the couch," and tied her hands behind her back.

The house was now absolutely silent. He wandered around it, wondering what he might steal. He opened the woman's purse lying on a table in the hall, but there was not a cent in it. He looked long and hard at the packed suitcase standing by the door but did not open it.

He felt himself getting more and more worked up. There was a strange sense of exultation in being master of the house. The man and woman were bound like slaves, his to do with as he wished. He was in command, in charge of their life and death, just as his mother and his stepfathers had been in charge of his life when he was a boy. He had always been the one to take orders. Now he was giving orders.

He knew that somehow he had to keep the man and woman silent. He could not take the risk that they would identify him. He looked at the shotgun in his hand. He could use that.

Then, in his stalking of the house, he saw a large knife on the kitchen table. He put down the gun, picked up the knife. He went back to the bedroom. He walked over to the farmer. He had the feeling someone else was doing it as he took the knife and cut the farmer's wrists, as once he had carefully cut his own wrist.

The farmer moaned, saying, "Oh, my God," his agonized eyes staring up helplessly at Ray; then his eyes closed as the blood started to drain out of his body. As though still only playing a part, Ray slit the farmer's throat, first from the left side to the middle, then from the right side to the middle.

He walked out of the room, leaving the little girl untouched in her small bed. He didn't think she saw what happened, even though she heard her father's moans. The bed stood under a window and faced a wall, so she would be looking at the wall or out the window, seeing only the trees.

He walked into the living room and over to the very pregnant, half-naked woman. Her eyes flicked in terror as he approached her, the knife dripping with her husband's blood. She gasped, "Please don't. Don't!" but that didn't stop him. He put down the knife, grabbed her around the neck, and tightened his fingers on her windpipe. Soon all breath was gone from her. He then cut her wrists and throat, as he had done her husband's.

He washed the bloody knife off in the kitchen sink and left it on a table. He started to walk out the back door, the door through which he had entered about three hours before when it was daylight. Now darkness enclosed him; he could barely see the outline of his white Ford on the dirt road.

As he stepped out the door he stumbled and fell into what seemed a pit. His leg snapped under him. He thought he might have broken it. But when he stood up he found he could walk. He limped to his car. The engine started up easily after the long wait. He turned the car around in that narrow dirt road and started back in the direction of his friend's home.

As he drove, he looked at his clothes. He was wearing a brown and white sports jacket, brown slacks, and a white shirt. There wasn't a spot of blood on them. He had done a neat job. He looked at his hands. They were clean too.

He stopped at a bar on the outskirts of town and had two beers. The television was on, and he listened. There was no news of any murders. Then he drove to the house where he was staying. The children were in bed; the husband, who had a night job at a factory, had gone to work, but the wife was awake.

"We were worried about you when you didn't show up for supper," she said. "Are you all right?"

"I'm all right," he said.

᚛᚛᚛᚛᚛᚛

He watched television all the next day at the house, but there was no news as yet of any murders in that area. Nor was there any that night.

But the day after, as he sat alone in the house, there came a report of the vicious, senseless slaughter of Mr. and Mrs. James Rogers at their farm in the presence of their little daughter.

He sat looking at a film of the scene at the farmhouse as the bodies, covered with white sheets, were carried out to the waiting ambulance.

He went into the bathroom and vomited.

Then he packed the few clothes he had brought, scribbled a note saying he was leaving, put it on the kitchen table, and walked out of the house. He stepped into his white Ford and headed south, away from Michigan, away from the little white farmhouse.

He made it to Florida. There, penniless, he decided to break into a small bar after it closed and try to find money enough to eat. He was caught.

Police all over the country had been alerted to be on the lookout for a man in a white Ford with Missouri license plates, wanted for the brutal murders in Michigan. The man in the truck who had stopped to give Ray water had furnished a good description of the stranger and his car. A sketch of the suspect had been circulated to all police departments. Fingerprints left on the shotgun and in the house were sent to the FBI to see if the killer had a record. It would be easy enough to match Ray's fingerprints with those on the gun and in the house.

He admitted the murders. He said he did not know why he had committed them. After he was brought back to Michigan, a sheriff asked, "What was going through your mind?"

He replied, "I can't say definitely because I don't know."

Asked if he remembered cutting the farmer's wrists, he said, "I remember cutting his wrists clearer than anything else that happened. By that time I was really psyched."

"Really in orbit, you mean," said the sheriff. "How did you feel afterward?"

"It was like a bad nightmare, like you are going to wake up any time."

Asked if he remembered cutting the wrists of the farmer's wife, he said, "No, I really don't. The reason why I do it that way is because I once cut my own wrists, and it didn't hurt."

The police learned that this mild-mannered, slender, almost scholarly looking man, who appeared much younger than his thirty-six years, had a record of at least seventeen burglaries and two assaults on women, one of them a vicious attack. He had been sentenced to a fifteen-year term in the Washington State Reformatory for grand larceny in 1956 but was discharged after serving two years. The next year he was sentenced to the Nevada State Prison for first degree burglary for a term of one to fifteen years but was discharged two years later. While in the Army, which he entered in 1955, he went AWOL and received an "undesirable" discharge while serving the prison term for grand larceny.

He had been charged with "assault with intent to ravish with malice" on May 8, 1964, in St. Louis, Missouri, an act that was described in the record as "practically a homicide" though the victim, Harriet Cantor, survived. The police report described the event:

> Cantor had a date with a girl friend to meet in a bar. When she arrived she and her girl friend had several drinks, and then Cantor went to her girl friend's apartment and they talked awhile. Cantor left the apartment to make a phone call from a telephone booth across the street. While she was in the booth a man whom she had seen in the tavern came into the booth, put his hand over her mouth, and told her that if she screamed he would kill her, at which time he dragged her and then told her to walk. . . . The man began choking her, and she fainted. When Cantor came to she felt something around her neck, which she discovered was her slip, which was spotted with blood. Her bra was lying on the ground with blood on it, at which time the man took her into the house and told her to call a cab and not the police or he would kill her. When the cab driver arrived, he put her into the cab.

After she arrived home, Mrs. Cantor called the police. Ray Boxer was caught and sentenced to six years in an institution of the Department of Corrections of Missouri after pleading guilty as charged.

※※※※※※

The Circuit Court of the state of Michigan, in session at the courthouse in the village of Cassopolis in the County of Cass, August 1974, appointed me as psychiatrist to the court to examine the defendant, Ray Boxer, to determine whether he was legally insane at the time of the murders of Mr. and Mrs. Rogers. He was charged with two counts of first degree murder and one count of manslaughter, the latter on the "term infant" within the body of the farmer's wife. She had been due to deliver the baby, a girl, at any moment. The packed suitcase had been hers, ready for the hospital.

Shortly after this, I received a letter from Ray Boxer's attorney, Jerry J. O'Connor, of the firm of O'Connor and Feldman, giving me information about Boxer's background. It included a report from the Diagnostic Center of the Division of Classification and Assignment of the Missouri Department of Corrections made in 1962, when Ray Boxer was twenty-four years old.

Mr. O'Connor described Ray as thirty-six years old, five feet, ten inches, 140 pounds, of slight build, brown eyes, and medium-length blond hair. He was born in Los Angeles. His family was Protestant. Mr. O'Connor also wrote: "He states that his father died when he was one; other sources state that the father abandoned the family."

I noticed that the report of the Diagnostic Center contained the information that his mother, in answering a questionnaire, stated, "His father was no good. I could take no more of his getting drunk and beating me, so when Ray was ten months old I left his father."

According to the report, his mother, by the time he was twenty-four years old, had subsequently married "at least three men [it eventually proved to be seven], each marriage involving displacement of the family and moving about to other parts of the country. He [Ray] expresses no concern for his mother's welfare and states that he has not seen her since 1958.''

> During his adolescence [the report continued], the accused was placed in a correctional institution in Oregon for car theft or joy riding. He did not graduate from high school, advancing only to the tenth grade. Various tests of Boxer administered by the Missouri Department of Corrections while he was imprisoned in Missouri showed that he was of above average intelligence.
> The accused has been convicted and imprisoned four times for the following crimes: grand larceny; burglary in the first degree; assault to do great bodily harm with malice; and assault with intent to ravish [the attack on Mrs. Cantor]. . . . While incarcerated in the Missouri State Prison for this offense, Boxer came into contact with a social worker and apparently received considerable help from her. He seemingly holds her in great respect and feels that she is one of the few persons that has ever given him help.
> After serving approximately one-half of his term on the last offense, Boxer was released in February 1968; he married shortly thereafter and settled into a satisfactory job. For the next two and a half years, Boxer lived a normal life and has stated that he felt more calm during this period than at any other time during his life. Approximately eight to twelve months ago, however, tension began to build, brought on in part by financial problems. According to Mrs. Boxer he became very nervous and continued to suffer from migraine headaches which had plagued him throughout the marriage. The headaches were very painful, and he would sit, unmoving, for as long as it took for the pain to subside. Mrs. Boxer also stated that he had feelings of sexual inadequacy at this time, which led to considerable tension between them. For some time prior to their separation on March 24, 1972, he forced his wife to have intercourse with him for two to three hours at a time. During this time he would have three to five orgasms and still not feel tired or satisfied. They separated when Mrs. Boxer learned from her 17-year-old daughter (by a previous marriage) that the daughter had been forcibly raped by Boxer.

During the latter part of 1971, he had been treated by a dentist. Treatment involved the prescribing of tranquilizers; Boxer had originally gone to the dentist because he was harming his jawbone by constant grinding of his teeth.

Boxer is skilled artistically; he is a self-taught painter and has painted extensively while in prison. He has a permanent exhibit of his paintings in an art gallery in Chicago. Enclosed are several works done while he has been imprisoned in the Cass County Jail. Four of the pictures contain trees; upon inquiring of Boxer as to why he often painted trees, he stated that he did so because they were easy. The picture of the junkyard is perhaps the most interesting; the chair, suitcase, washing machine and bed headboard found in the picture closely resemble items found in the home of the slain couple. The wife had packed a suitcase in preparation for leaving for the hospital.

◈◈◈◈◈◈◈◈

I reserved the entire afternoon of August 25 to interview Ray Boxer. I had studied the four paintings sent by the attorney and was surprised at their high degree of artistic skill. One thing stood out glaringly: all the trees he painted had broken limbs, symbolizing, I thought, how he felt—broken, castrated. It was significant that in his painting of a junkyard, done while he was in the county jail, there was a suitcase, a chair, a washing machine, and a bed headboard. A painting may be like a projective test, telling what disturbs the artist.

Ray Boxer was brought to my office well guarded, to make sure he would not try to escape. I knew what he would look like from Mr. O'Connor's description. He was slender, with a boyish face and the sensitive features of an artist. His voice was rather high-pitched, but it had a detached tone. He spoke slowly and sometimes in poor English.

I began by asking, "Tell me what are you charged with."

He said, "Two counts of murder and one manslaughter."

"How did that come about? There were three victims?"

"A man and wife and an unborn child," he said. Then he

added, "Do you want to know about the crime itself, or do you want to know about leading up to it?"

"I want to know about both," I said.

"It was a lot of things that led up to it, that's why I asked. Before I came to Michigan I lost my job and everything we had, and then I lost my family—we split up. After all this happened I was just lost, but I happen to have a couple of friends who lived up here in Michigan. I didn't know what to do or where to go, so I just took off up here to see them. I was running around job hunting every day while I was up here. One afternoon, the day that this thing happened, I had been job hunting. Anyway, I stopped along this road and I was broke, I didn't have any money, and there was this old house back up the road. I walked up to it. The front door was locked, so I went around to the back door. I was no more than inside and the people drove up, so I was stuck in there, see? I didn't know what to do, so I just stepped in a closet, and all the time I was just getting keyed up, you know. So I stayed in there quite some time. Right outside there was a shotgun on the wall, so I took that shotgun and stepped in there and confronted them with it. I was scared, so I faced him with the shotgun."

"You pointed the shotgun at whom?"

"At both of them. I told them to come in and sit down. They had a little child there, a little girl. I don't know how old she was, maybe five, something like that."

"She was walking?"

"Oh, yes."

"Was she talking?"

"No. I don't remember her ever saying anything."

"So you pointed the shotgun and made them go into the living room."

"Because I just didn't know what to do, see? The woman was making coffee at the time, so we just sat there and drank coffee for about three hours, I guess. Like I say, I was scared and worked up."

"Were you talking about anything?"

"No, we didn't talk much. I was trying to figure out what I was going to do."

"What kind of possibilities did you have? What could you have done?"

"I don't know. I don't have any idea. Even now I can't think of any."

"What happened next? You say you drank coffee for about three hours and no conversation took place?"

"Very little. She wanted to feed the little girl, so I let her feed her. She went in the kitchen."

"What did you do during that time?"

"I just kept getting keyed up by the minute, that's all."

"You sat there with her husband, is that right?"

"Yes. So then later I finally tied them up, tied him onto the middle bed, you know, and I tied her hands, and I really don't remember a lot."

"What did you use to tie him?"

"I think I took his shoelaces; he was wearing boots, so he had rawhide shoelaces. I tied him on his back with his hands up to the bedstead."

"He made no attempt to fight you or escape?"

"No, how could he? I had the shotgun on him all the time."

"When you tied him you had to put the shotgun down, didn't you?"

"Yeah, briefly."

"So you tied him in a different room?"

"Yeah, a little bedroom off to the side."

"Then you went ahead and tied her?"

"Tied her hands behind her."

"Where was she at the time? Which room?"

"In the living room. The doorway to the bedroom's right there. I could see him all the time."

"What about the little girl?"

"I didn't tie her up or anything. I told the police I thought I remembered putting her in the bed, a baby bed there, but I don't really remember."

"What happened then?"

"I was just crazy. My mind was ringing, my heartbeat was going ninety miles an hour. I stepped out of the kitchen door. I like to broke my leg. I remember that. I remember falling. I don't know why. It was like the floor just wasn't there. Then I was back in the car."

"What happened to the people left there?"

"What happened to them? I killed them, I guess."

"How did you kill them?"

"The police said their wrists and their throats were cut."

"They were not shot?"

"No."

"Why would that be, since you had a shotgun?"

"I really don't know. Maybe it's like I told the under-sheriff—that there's no pain that way. So maybe that's why I did it. I know there isn't any pain because I cut my wrists a few years ago."

"What happened to the little girl?"

"Not a thing."

"You mean she witnessed it?"

"I don't know. I don't know that she did. If I put her in that baby bed, she wouldn't have been in there. I don't know. I can't really say."

"We do have to make a distinction as to what you know about it now and what you remember. I would like you to tell me now what you yourself remember."

"I remember cutting his wrist. I remember tying him up and then walking around and around and around. I didn't bother anything. I didn't rummage the house or anything. I just walked . . . maybe an hour, thirty minutes, I don't know . . . just walked, around and around. You see, I was getting all keyed up. I get keyed up real easy anyway."

"When you say you were 'keyed up,' were you kind of scared? Is that what you mean by keyed up? Or nervous?"

"I was probably scared."

"What were you scared about?"

"I don't know."

"You had them tied up, you had the shotgun, you had a car. What were you scared of? Try to remember. What feelings did you have?"

"I don't know."

"Tell me whatever comes to your mind even if it doesn't make any sense."

"Well, see, for some time I've been worked up anyway. I lost everything I had. I got screwed on my job. My employer owed me almost four years of royalties, and he screwed me out of that, and I stuck with him. My family went without. I worked weekends and many, many overtime hours, never getting paid for it—all on promises."

"What employer?"

"I worked for a plastics company. And all the time I'm doing this, my wife was going through cancer operations, I'm paying for that too, no company insurance. Bankrupt, lost everything we had. Finally my employer wanted me to work three days a week, so I quit. So we didn't have any money, trying to move, trying to find another house. We just couldn't make it anymore. So I just blew my family life up."

"That was in St. Louis?"

"Yes."

"How did you happen to get to this area?"

"I was loose. I didn't know where to go or what to do, and I happened to have some old friends that came up here from St. Louis."

"It's not clear to me how you happened to walk into that house. You were driving and you saw the house just off the road?"

"It's an old gravel road, a dirt road."

"What were you doing on that old gravel road?"

"I'd been running around the little towns right around there job hunting, putting in applications."

"Were you living in Michigan for any length of time?"

"I lived there about three weeks with these friends of mine. I've known them for years. I met the man's brother through some trouble I was in."

"You met him where? In jail?"

"Yes."

"So you saw the farmhouse and you went inside. What time of day was it?"

"Late in the afternoon. About five."

"Was it dark outside?"

"No."

"Why did you go inside?"

"I don't know. I think I had an idea I might find some money or something."

"From what you describe, it didn't sound like a house that would have a lot of money in it. But you hoped there might be some?"

"Yes. See, I wasn't out to try to make a big killing. I hadn't been up to any criminal activities."

"You say you talked to the farmer and his wife for about three hours. That would put it at around eight o'clock. By that time it was dark, wasn't it?"

"Yes, roughly."

"It was getting dark. Let's go back where we left off. I want you to tell me what you remember. You said you remembered cutting his wrist. What did you use?"

"A knife out of the kitchen. A paring knife of some kind. That's all I remember. The police say their throats were cut. I don't remember cutting their throats. And they said his arm was cut on the inside. I don't remember that."

"Do you know the people's names?"

"I don't remember it. I keep hearing it in court."

"Do you remember doing anything to the woman?"

"No, I don't."

"Do you remember cutting the man's wrist, one or both?"

"I don't know if I remember cutting both of them. But I can remember one of them just as clear as a bell."

"What did you think at the time that you did it?"

"Just a bad dream. Like you're going to wake up and it's— you know. By that time I was gone anyway. I couldn't believe it afterward. I stopped at the edge of town. There's a bar there. I couldn't believe it. I went in there and got a beer and sat down at the end of the bar, and I was just as clean. I wasn't bloody or nothing. I was wearing nice clothes. A white shirt."

"You couldn't believe what?"

"I couldn't really believe that I'd done this. I couldn't believe it. And I had no signs of it."

"What did you decide had happened?"

"I just—like I say, a bad dream. You're going to wake up and it's all over with. I sat all the next day in front of that television watching the news and listening to the radio, and I didn't hear anything on the news."

"What were you listening for?"

"Possibly about that. Because like I said, I couldn't really believe it."

"You were listening on the assumption that you would hear something about this, so you knew something had happened. Did you think they might not discover the bodies?"

"I don't think I really even thought about that. But I know all day there was nothing. It was like the next day—bingo!"

"It was on the news the next day?"

"Yeah. And then I was sick."

"When you say sick, you mean what?"

"Physically sick. I threw up and I couldn't eat."

"What did they say on the news?"

"That they'd been found, that's all."

"Did they give any other details?"

"Yeah, enough that I knew that that's what it was, because it was near Cassopolis."

"You mean, up until hearing it on the news you had some doubts?"

"You mean as to what happened? Well, yeah, sure I did."

"Explain it to me. I would like to understand. How could you have doubts, since you remembered?"

"Because I couldn't remember doing all of this, see? Like I couldn't remember what happened to her or the kid or how I got out. I couldn't even remember getting out."

"Did you take anything from the house?"

"No."

"What happened to the shotgun?"

"It's still there, I guess. I didn't have it afterward."

"What did you do after you came to the bar? Do you remember what you ordered to drink?"

"Same thing I always do. I'm not a heavy drinker. Beer."

"Did you spend any length of time in the bar?"

"I think I stayed there a half hour, forty-five minutes maybe."

"Did you talk to anybody?"

"No."

"Tell me anything else that comes to your mind about it."

"Well, really, that's about all. I didn't know what to do then, so I just took off."

"You took off from where?"

"From Michigan. I just got in the car and took off."

"Where did you go?"

"I just left for the South. Stopped in Nashville and Gatlinburg, stopped by Fort Campbell, Kentucky. These are all places I've been or been stationed. I was going on down to Florida because that's where my wife and I spent one vacation. By the time I got down there I didn't have any money again. I tried to break in a little bar that was way up by itself and got caught. So then they came down and got me."

"How did they find out you were the one responsible for the death of the two people?"

"I don't know. There was a guy that saw my car parked down the road from that house, and he stopped while I was standing at the car, before I went in the house, and he asked me if I was having car trouble. I said, yeah, I thought it was hot, you know. I'm no mechanic, so that's what I thought. That was the first reason I stopped to begin with, because you let the car set like that every once in a while and then it would start up again and be all right, see? He gave me some water he had, a jug of water. So I went to put some water in, but it didn't take but just a little bit, so it wasn't that. It wasn't boiling over or anything."

"So this guy had a chance to talk to you and take a good look at you. He was the man who described you to the police then?"

"Yes. Plus the fact that I had a white Ford and southern plates."

"You must have also left fingerprints on the shotgun."

"I don't know about that."

"Did you do anything to remove fingerprints from the shotgun?"

"Not that I know of."

"You were around the house and you handled a knife and a shotgun. You would have left fingerprints, you know. It's like leaving your address."

"That's what I told the police. I don't remember wiping that stuff. It's logical that I would have wiped it off, yeah. If I'd been absolutely aware of what I was doing, I know I would have."

"So you were apprehended for the robbery of the bar, or rather for the attempted break-in—actually you did break in, didn't you?"

"And they contacted the FBI, and the FBI notified the police up here. They came down and got me."

"Tell me, what do you think of all that?"

"What do I think about it? I try not to."

"But at the same time I'm sure you must at times think about it. How did it happen."

"Oh, yeah, I've thought about it a lot."

"So what do you come up with?"

"I really don't know, because it's not like me. It's not a thing like me. Because I'm too sensitive. I get hurt too easily myself. I've always been that way."

"Tell me about yourself generally. You are how old?"

"I'm thirty-six. I was born in Salem, Oregon."

"Give me a little description of your early life and yourself, as if you were writing your own biography."

"You haven't got time."

"Don't worry about my time. I have time."

"You see, I was all over the country."

"Start kind of early and tell me about your parents, and I'll ask you questions. But start on your own."

"My real dad died when I was a year old. He fell in an ice pit and then got an infection in the bones of his legs. That's all I know. He lived about a year in a wheelchair and then died. Since then I've had seven stepdads, the last count. I haven't seen my mother since '58, just before Christmas. I lived briefly here in Detroit when I was a kid, when I was just in grade school. I had some grandfolks lived here, on my dad's side, and they sent me to military school in Monroe, Michigan, for a few years.

"But then my mother, she got divorced and got married again, and she come after me or sent for me. So then she'd get divorced again, so I'd be sent back here to my grandfolks again. So they'd talk them into taking me back at the military school. Then the last time, my mother showed up about midnight one night and just literally kidnapped me from there. See, my granddad wasn't going to send me back again, wasn't going to let her have me. So she showed up.''

"You mean your mother was married seven times? These changes were in what span of time, up to what age? You say your natural father died when you were one year old?''

"Up till I was about seventeen, eighteen, I guess, cause I went in the Army then. So I lived all over the country. I've been in almost every state in the United States when I was just a kid. My folks traveled all the time.''

"Your folks—meaning who?''

"My various stepfathers and my mother.''

"Tell me about the first stepfather.''

"I don't remember much about him. The first two I don't know much about because I was too young.''

"What about the third one?''

"I can't tell you what he did. I lived with him briefly. I lived with my grandfolks on my mother's side while I was with him. I can't tell you what he did for a living. Briefly, we lived right outside Little Rock, Arkansas, and he bought an old store and filling station, and he was going to fix it all up, but he never did. That's about all I remember of him.''

"What about the next one?''

"He was a carpenter and a heavy drinker. But I didn't live too much with him, so I don't know too much about him. I tell you, my first stepdad that I really know quite a bit about was the third. He ran heavy equipment, I think. We did a lot of moving around, I know that. Then the next one, the fourth, he was a booze hound and an engineer for Southern Pacific Railroad. He's an ex-Navy man. Really thought he was it.''

"What about your mother? What kind of a person was she?''

"Well, my mother and I never were really too close. I don't know, I never could figure Mom out. She's not a runaround or anything like that, yet all those marriages might make you think, you know. But she never was. She never did chase around or do a lot of drinking or anything.''

"Tell me about your military experiences.''

"Well, I liked that. I was in the Army Airborne Paratroopers. I took my boot training at Fort Campbell.''

"Did that go all right?"

"Yeah, I loved it. I was in about two years, I guess, and then I flubbed up, messed up. I had a good record. I was in the Division Band and Honor Guard."

"What instrument did you play in the band?"

"The clarinet and sax. They'd fly us around for parades in different parts of the country, and I really liked that. I guess I liked that regiment—inspections and all that stuff. They never bothered me. Like I say, I had a good record, so I got it in my head I was going to run off AWOL for a weekend and hop to Nevada because my mother had just been married again. I was going to fly out and see her and fly back, see? Well, I got out there and couldn't get a hop back, so they sent me up to Fort Lewis, Washington."

He had gone AWOL to see his mother, I recalled, when she had remarried for what would be the fifth or sixth time.

"Up to the time you went into the military at the age of seventeen, had you any difficulties with the law?" I asked.

"Yeah, I was in trouble when I went in."

"Is that the reason why you went in?"

"No. I was in trouble just before that. I wasn't in trouble at the time I went in."

"What was the first offense you had of any kind?"

"I was just a kid, a freshman in high school, I guess, up in Oregon. A friend of mine, his dad or his uncle, I don't remember which now, owned a bar, tavern, and dance hall right there in Oak Ridge, and it stuck out over the bank over the river. We used to clean it up for him. My friend showed me how to get in there at night. So we started swiping a little beer here and there, goodies like bags of potato chips and all that. Then he found out about it, so they arrested us. So they stuck me in a detention home because I didn't have any parents here at the time, because mother had just moved."

"How old were you when this happened?"

"Fourteen. I was staying with a friend and his family to finish out school."

"Where was your mother at the time?"

"She left with her husband. I don't know where they went then."

"Who paid for your food and lodging?"

"I did. I worked in the meat market after school and on weekends."

"So at the age of fourteen you were self-sustaining?"

"Yeah."

Not many boys have to support themselves at the age of fourteen, I thought, nor do many, luckily, have a mother who abandons them so often and at such an early age, which can only provoke great wrath in a child.

"What was the next offense in which you were involved? Was there one before the military? You mentioned one shortly before you entered."

"There was that one, they put me in a detention home. Then I broke out of the detention home and swiped a car. So it just snowballed. After they first arrested me, it just snowballed. I broke out of there and swiped a car, then they brought me back and they threatened they were going to send me to prison and all that stuff. I was scared and I broke out again and swiped a car, cause I was scared, you know, at fourteen, that they were going to put me in prison. I traveled at night, and I'd break into filling stations that were closed. I never got anything but a handful of change, but it bought my gas and kept me going. Then they caught me and sent me to Woodburn Reformatory."

"Is that in Oregon?"

"Yeah. I don't remember how long I spent there. A year and a half, maybe. By that time my mother was married again, and they were living on a farm up in Iowa, so I came up there and started working on the farm, working for farmers around the area. And then I went in the Army."

"What happened after the Army?"

"Just trouble after trouble. See, when I went AWOL, that time they sent me up to Fort Lewis. I had had a good record; they weren't going to court-martial me, but they wouldn't send me back. They wouldn't put me in an airborne outfit; they were just going to leave me there in a leg outfit. I was in the paratroopers, and I happened to be damn proud of it at the time."

"Why?"

"Because I liked it."

"What did you like about it?"

"I liked the jumping. I liked the fellows I met. I liked the pride."

"What's so great about jumping from a plane? It's pretty dangerous."

"Everybody wouldn't do it."

"It sounds kind of risky, doesn't it?"

"It is, to an extent, yeah."

"But you say you liked it?"

"I loved it."

"What did you love about it?"

"I just loved that routine, I guess. I don't know."

"Did you make many jumps?"

"Oh, yeah. I jumped when I didn't have to. You're only required to jump once every three months."

"And you jumped more often than that?"

"Yeah, I jumped every month if I could. You had to get on a roster to do it. You'd go around and find out who was jumping and where, and if there was room for you, you could get on, see? But if you didn't do that every time, you'd jump every ninety days. It's just like the first time all over again. I loved it. I had fun at it."

"Do you like situations where there's some risk involved?"

"I don't know."

"Did you ever gamble?"

"No, never have."

"What happened after you left the military?"

"Like I said, they weren't going to court-martial me, but they weren't going to put me back in an airborne outfit, either. I didn't like Fort Lewis. Colder than hell. So I left and I stole a car and got caught. Then I went to the penitentiary."

"Which penitentiary?"

"In Nevada."

"How long were you in the penitentiary?"

"I got one to fifteen years. I think I pulled about eighteen months."

"When you got out of the service you were about nineteen or twenty?"

"About twenty, I guess."

"And then you spent not quite two years in Nevada in the penitentiary, so you were about twenty-two, is that right?"

"Right."

"What happened next?"

"Well, I stayed there and worked awhile in Nevada, and then my mother and her fourth husband went to Omaha. So then I went up to Omaha and got a job, rented an apartment. Got a job landscaping the same place he was working. Then, I don't know, some time later I came to Missouri and got in trouble right away."

"What kind of trouble?"

"Burglary."

"What happened?"

"I was broke, didn't have a job, couldn't find a job. I got caught on a burglary. They sent me to Jefferson City."

"For how long?"

"I don't remember. Seems like I got two years, three years, something like that."

"What happened after you were discharged?"

"I got out and went to work in St. Louis. I worked for a matrix company. Got to drinking and chasing around till finally I got in trouble again."

"For what?"

"An assault charge, assault with intent to ravish."

"You mean you tried to rape a woman, is that it?"

"No. See, I was in a bar right across the street from where I lived, and these two women came in. They started making all up to me. I don't associate with people a hell of a lot. When I go to a bar, I don't go around talking to everybody. But they came right to me, wanting to dance, playing the juke box. Well, this one lived across the street just about two houses from where I was living, and she's really egging me on, you know, and like I say, we were drinking and I can't hold a lot. Anyway, she was gonna go home with the other gal and then come back, but after a while I just had all I could drink. When I got outside, I ran right into her. So we walked across on the other side and got into a big argument. I don't know exactly what it was about or anything. Anyway, I guess I jumped her or choked her or something. That's what she said in court."

"That is not what she said."

"Yeah, it was."

"No. Not at least from what I have read."

"She said that I tried to assault her. That I tried to rape her."

"No, she said she was in a telephone booth and you came in and you put your hand on her mouth and told her you would kill her if she didn't keep quiet. Isn't that what she said?"

"Oh, no. No. No. That's not true."

"All I am saying is what I have read in the record. Isn't that what she said? That's what's described."

"Well, it might be. Because we didn't go to trial. I'm just saying that's not true. I really don't know what she said."

"What she said was that while she was in a telephone booth a man whom she had seen in the tavern before came into the booth, put his hand over her mouth, and told her that if she screamed he would kill her, at which time he dragged her and then told her to walk, which she did, until they reached the rear yard of such and such a street, and then the man began choking her and she fainted. And when she came to she felt something around her neck and she discovered it was her slip which was spotted with blood, and her bra was lying on the ground full of blood. Remember that?"

"No. But it never started that way. I met her out on the sidewalk. The telephone booths are right there on the corner."

"Do you remember putting something around her neck?"

"No. But her husband was in a hospital or something."

"Yes. She said she was on her way to visit her husband, and then went to the bar with a friend."

"She called him in the telephone booth, and then we went on across the street."

"So then you went to prison. How long did you stay there?"

"Six years I think they sentenced me."

"How much time did you serve?"

"I really can't tell you."

"A year or two?"

"It was better than two years, I know, because you have to do a third."

"What was the next thing as far as trouble with the law is concerned?"

"That's it."

"There is one more where you attacked a woman with a knife."

"In Missouri?"

" 'The subject pointed a pocket knife at Eleanor Burns with the intent to do great bodily harm to her,' " I read from the report. "What was that?"

"Oh, yeah. That was just a crazy mixed-up affair."

"Tell me about it."

"There isn't a heck of a lot I can tell you. I was drinking across the street from the bus depot and I just piled in the car with them. They wanted to take me somewhere. I don't remember where—been too long ago. Like I said, I was drunk, that's all it amounted to. It wasn't just one woman, either; there were several in the car."

"According to this report there was a woman and her daughter."

"There were two grown women and kids in that car."

"Do you think of the fact that you have had frequent problems with the law throughout your life?"

"I don't know why."

"Have you reflected about it?"

"Yeah. I don't know what the root of it is. Because I'm a good worker. I've never in my life been fired from a job."

"But you don't get a chance to work for a very long period before you get put in jail. You have been in jail many times, haven't you? Since the age of fourteen, how much time have you spent in jail?"

"I don't know, but if I hadn't been on my own, if I'd had any help, I wouldn't have been in all them times. Right from the start the judge sentenced me because I was by myself. I had nobody to help me. That was the only reason."

"Aside from this recent tragedy, have you ever hurt anybody?"

"No."

"Yes, you did. One woman, you know."

"Yeah, well, you know about that. I guess I choked her. I didn't kill her or anything."

"You told me you cut your own wrist. When did that happen? In fact, I can see it. Let me take another look at your wrist."

"Yeah, I did a good job."

"It certainly looks like you did. What did you use?"

"A razor blade. I cut the tendons to them fingers." He pointed to his index and fourth finger on his right hand.

"When did this happen?"

"When I was in jail in Missouri. I wanted them to give me some help."

"What do you mean by 'help'?"

"Psychiatric help. They said they would, so I cooperated right down the line."

"Meaning what?"

"I tell them anything they want to know. So the next thing I know they sentence me to Jeff City. Big deal—that's going to give me a lot of help." Sarcastically.

"You mean you confessed to all the crimes you committed?"

"Yeah. They never in the world could have pinned that on me," referring to the assault case.

"In fact, as I recall from reading the material, you, to use your term, 'cleaned up' seventeen cases, is that right?"

"Yep. See, they were really gonna help me and instead they put the shaft in, that's what they did. Prison doesn't scare me. I look at prison the same way as I do out here."

"What do you mean?"

"One's just about the same as the other. I pick my little groove and I stay in it. Prison doesn't bother me. They say you can't ride the fence, but I do it."

"In prison, you mean?"

"Yeah. I don't like the convicts in there. Out here I don't like most of the people I meet because everybody's out to do you in, hurt you in some way or use you. So when I'm in there, I pick my little groove. Like the last time it was art. I mean I dug into it. I started studying a lot harder than any student would outside because I worked around the clock."

"I have to say the work you have done—I have four samples of it—is beautiful."

"That's nothing. I've got stuff in permanent exhibit in Chicago."

I took out the paintings and showed him the junkyard scene. "What brought this to mind—this 'no dumping' scene?"

"I don't know."

"You did this just from memory?"

"I do all my stuff like that. That's just piddling little stuff."

"What do you call it?"

"Just sketches."

"What do you use to do this?"

"Those are felt-tip pens."

"You do so many trees."

"Well, I did when I first started. That's because my nerves were shaking. You can always do trees then. You don't need any fine lines."

"There are many fine lines in these trees. But there's something else about these trees that does impress me. As you look at them—one, two, three, and four, including this one"—I pointed to them—"what is outstanding about them, aside from being artistic?"

He looked blank.

"The trees all seem to be broken, or something is broken in the picture," I said. "Not one of them seems to be a regular kind of tree, right?"

"Because they're old?"

"No. I mean they all seem to have broken branches."

"Sure, that lends interest to it. You know, if you're going to draw a barn or something, you don't draw a perfect straight, nice, beautiful, even barn; you hang a door, take a board off here and there, to give it interest."

"I see." I changed the subject, a threatening one to him. "You said prison doesn't scare you, but why did you cut your wrists? It looks like you made a very serious suicidal attempt."

"I meant to, and I damn near made it."

"Had you ever tried suicide before?"

"No."

"How about since?"

"I thought about it a lot of times. I would have done it this time if I hadn't got caught, probably, because it was in my mind every day."

"You mean before you got caught after the killings?"

"No, before that."

"Why were you going to commit suicide before the killings?"

"Because I lost everything I had. I lost everything I worked for. I lost my family, my job, everything."

"Let's talk about your marriage. That was your first marriage, wasn't it?"

"Yes."

"Tell me about it."

"Well, we just never had a chance, that's all. Right from the start. Just before I got married we had a pretty nice little thing going. I just had a sellout showing."

"Where was that?"

"In a big seminary in St. Louis. I won a big, distinguished award. This was 1967 or 1968."

"So you were pretty successful in art?"

"Yeah. I was on interviews on television, and I was selling everything I could do. Then I gave it up to get married."

"Tell me about your wife. How did you meet her?"

"The two people that I came up to Niles to see—Jerry and Dora—well, my wife was a friend of Dora's, and she was married at the time. She had been married ten years, but it was a bad affair. I met her, and we hit it off right away. I never intended to get married. I never thought about marriage."

"How did you get along with women generally?"

"Good. I never had trouble with any women. I get along better with women than I do men. Men I don't trust worth a damn. I've always got along with women."

"How did you get along sexually with women?"

"Good. I don't have any trouble."

"How old was your wife at the time you met her?"

"She's about nine months older than I am."

"You said you were not interested in marriage. What made you decide to get married?"

"I just don't know. It's just one of them things. I fell for her."

"Was she interested in marriage?"

"Oh, yeah."

"Was it her idea to get married or yours?"

"It was mine. I pushed it all the way."

"So you got married in 1968?"

"Yeah. September would have made six years."

"She was previously married and had children?"

"She had one daughter."

"And she got a divorce?"

"I got her a divorce. She didn't have the money to get it. Then we got married."

"How did things go in marriage?"

"Great. In the first year and a half it was really good."

"What happened then?"

"Buying things and making good money, on my way up, and then, by that time, I really got tied down with obligations. That's when the plastics company I was working for started going down. They got involved in a big swindle."

"If your art was going so well, why did you work for the plastics company?"

"Because I couldn't make it in art. You can't count on a paycheck every week."

"You say the marriage was going fine, so what led to the breakup?"

"My job. Like I said, the company, after I was there about two years, got involved in a swindle and a lawsuit."

"What were you doing for them?"

"I started out as just a caster, casting molds and things like that. Then I moved to a foreman, then a lead man, then I was assistant plant superintendent. All in three and a half years. Wasn't anybody that could handle that plastic like I did. I had about forty pieces that were my stuff, sold right there. Sculpture and wall décor items that I designed."

"How did your marriage breakup come about?"

"Well, I told you she went through a couple of cancer operations."

"Where was the cancer?"

"In her tubes. The second time she had a complete hysterectomy. Our big trouble was financial. It just drove us in the ground. We just couldn't get out, there wasn't any way of getting out. We were living in a new home we were going to buy, and we were behind with payments. Then we borrowed to try to straighten things out, and that never helps, just makes it worse. So finally we didn't have any money, and clear down to the last, the boss was wanting me to work three days a week, get paid for three days but work six or seven days, all for the company. So finally I just quit. I found a flunky job; it was the only thing I could find."

"Who filed for divorce?"

"Nobody yet. She's still my wife."

"So you left her, is that right?"

"She's still in St. Louis."

"Did you discuss it or did you just pick up and leave?"

"We had a big row."

"Tell me about it."

"Well, we'd been fighting off and on quite a bit at the last. Maybe because of my own pride, being lost and everything. Then she wanted to go back to work, and she did, and that really socked it to me."

"Why? What were your objections to her working?"

"She wasn't supposed to be working. She didn't have a doctor's release in the first place, and in the second place I didn't want her working."

"You mean you don't feel a wife should work?"

"No."

"What was the row about?"

"Debt and money problems. We were just both on edge. I started drinking."

"Was there a fight?"

"We had several, not real bad, fights."

"Did you hit her?"

"No."

"So it was just a verbal fight. Then what? You took up and left or what?"

"One day I was off work and drinking, and my daughter's almost eighteen, that is, my stepdaughter. Like I said, I was drinking all day. I came home and had a couple more, then I guess I forced her—you know."

"You forced her to have sexual relations with you. How did you force her?"

"I just took her. There wasn't any problem to it."

"How did your sexual relations with your wife go?"

"It went good until the last year, I guess."

"Wasn't there some problem about you insisting on having intercourse for a long period of time?"

"What do you mean? I don't understand what you mean."

"I mean you would just go on for hours."

"Oh, no. No. Just one time that happened. You know, a lot of that was just hate."

"I don't understand. Explain what you mean by hate."

"I don't know how to explain it. You know, when you're mad—like you're getting even."

"Through intercourse you get even?"

"Yeah."

"Generally when people have intercourse they don't use it as a way of getting even. Could you maintain an erection for such a long period of time even if you were mad?"

"I did that once. That's not like an awful long time, you know."

"Did you have feelings of hate toward your wife?"

"No, not really. Just from all the scrapping, and feelings over the length of time going downhill. Her telling me she didn't care about sex."

"Was the pregnant woman you killed attractive?"

"I don't know."

"Did you make any sexual moves toward her?"

"No. They said she didn't have her bottoms on. She had a pair of kind of blue corduroy things on, I think. But she hadn't been assaulted or anything."

"Who removed her undergarments?"

"I don't know, unless I did."

"How do you know she wasn't assaulted? Maybe you did."

"I was going by what they said in court, the medical examiner."

"You mean the doctor who did the autopsy. Yes, but all he could tell was whether you had an ejaculation inside her. You could have made some sexual advances toward her. He couldn't tell this. I'm asking if you remember anything."

"No."

"Was she the kind of woman who would interest you?"

"I couldn't accurately describe her."

"You could tell that she was pregnant?"

"Yes."

"How did you feel about that?"

"If I told you, you'd think I was silly. Like you feel toward any pregnant woman."

"I rarely feel that anybody is silly, so tell me what you feel."

"You feel tenderness toward a pregnant woman. I always did. I always thought it was cute. I just said it sounds silly because of what I'd done, that's all."

"I'm used to seeing contradictory feelings in people, so I'm not at all disbelieving that you felt tender toward her."

"I didn't have any hate for those people."

There was a long pause. He had tears in his eyes, the first sign of guilt over his crimes, I thought.

Then he said gruffly, "I don't like this bullshit any more than anybody else does."

Murder to him was "bullshit," I noted; messing up, ejecting "dirty" matter.

"You mean what happened?" I asked.

"Yeah. That's why I try not to think about it."

"I can well accept that you don't like what happened."

"I've always thought about it—maybe that's why I can't remember it. Maybe everything inside of me is just fighting it, you know. Honest, I can't remember. There are parts, like breaking my leg, that I do remember."

"Did you break your leg?"

"No, but I damn sure could have. I keep talking about it because I don't know what happened. I don't know where I was. I just was aware of falling, like you stepped off in a big old hole in the house."

"You did say that you cut his wrist first. But she must have heard or seen it. Did she scream, do you remember?"

"I don't remember her screaming."

"But a person would scream if somebody cuts his or her wrists, or her husband's. There must have been a tremendous amount of screaming. I would assume that. Do you recall any?"

"No."

"When you cut his wrist, did he scream?"

"Maybe he said something about 'Oh, my God' or something. I don't know. I'm not trying to play any games."

"I don't think you are. There'd be no purpose in it, anyway, because not remembering is in no way of any value to you. I'm just trying to help you and get a better understanding of what happened."

"I don't understand myself. Like I say, it's not like me. Now you look at all that fouled-up record and maybe you might say—but I speak from what's inside, see? I hurt too easy myself. Constantly people are hurting me, see? I can't see myself doing it," referring to the murders.

"You can't see yourself doing it because you're not likely to hurt people, is that what you mean?"

"No, because I'm too sensitive toward hurt. Maybe I cut them because I know it didn't hurt, you know. As bad as I cut myself, through everything, all the veins and arteries—I cut the tendons to them fingers, and they had to fish down and get all the tendons—it never hurt. You just bleed and bleed and bleed until it's like going to sleep. You get weak."

"Have you ever knifed anybody before?"

"No. No."

"Are you likely to get into fights physically?"

"No, I've never been in fights. I say never, though I may have when I was a kid."

"How about in jail?"

"Never in jail. I have never been reprimanded in jail, never spent a day in solitary. A day in solitary would crack me up anyway."

"Have you ever been seen by a psychiatrist?"

"No. Except a couple in penitentiaries."

"You mean just for evaluation?"

"Yeah, but they're looney themselves."

"What do you mean?"

"Just what I said. They're looney. They need help too. I know one in Oregon's a homosexual, and he takes pills to stand up all day. Now you tell me he's fit to tell me what's wrong with me?"

"I notice a tattoo on your arm." A rose and dagger were etched on his outer upper right arm.

"I put that on when I was about fourteen or fifteen."

"You put it on yourself?"

"Yeah."

"Anything else you would like to tell me that we haven't touched on?"

"No, not that I can think of. It's just that going to the penitentiary is not going to do me any good. It's not like I'm trying to get out of it, because I'm not. Damn, I deserve to be hung. I know that."

"Why is that?"

"Because of the offense."

"What do you think should happen to you?"

"I'd like to get committed."

"Committed to what?"

"An institute where I can get some help. Counseling."

"You couldn't be committed, you know. You are being charged with a serious crime, and you could be sent to a hospital, but that would not be like a commitment."

"You mean I'd be in a very maximum security?"

"No, I don't mean that. If your lawyer and you decided that you should plead insanity, then even if the jury or the judge found you 'not guilty by virtue of insanity,' you would be sent to a state hospital that deals with people who have committed a crime. You are probably familiar with which one that is in this state, aren't you?"

"No, I'm not. I don't know anything about this state."

"Haven't you talked about it in jail with other fellows?"

"I don't talk to anybody. I've been by myself ever since I'm there."

"You don't mix with the other prisoners? How come?"

"I don't know. I like it that way."

"What do you think would happen if you did go to a mental institution?"

"Maybe get some counseling."

"What would that mean?"

"Oh, boy, I don't know. I don't know what you mean by these questions. I mean, you're talking about something I don't know a thing about."

"I know you don't know, but I'm trying to get from you how you picture it."

"I don't care what it's like, not if I can get some help, some counseling. And I wouldn't give a damn if it took fifty years, if it would help me. If not, going to the penitentiary isn't going to do me any good, and there's no sense in living if there or anywhere else a guy's not going to get some help. I've screamed help for better than ten years."

I asked, "What is it you would want help with? Suppose you came to see me as a patient, I would ask you what it is you would like to have changed, what's wrong with you? Aside from the murders—forget about this act for a moment—what would you tell me is wrong with you?"

"What's wrong with me? Well, there's a lot of things wrong with me. I'm overly sensitive to the fact that I get all keyed up and worked up just talking to some people. I've been so lonely I wanted to die all my life, but still I shun people. I get depressed, I get so damned depressed I want to crawl off and die, for no reason, just all of a sudden start bawling and feel sad, feel lonely. You can't tell me that's normal. When I was the happiest in my married life I still did the same thing. I'd want to crawl off and start bawling, but I'd crawl off to the basement or go out in the garage."

"And do what?"

"Just get by myself, so my wife wouldn't see it. She'd ask me, 'What's wrong, what's wrong?' I'd tell her, 'Nothing, just leave me alone and let it go.' I'd get over it and wouldn't talk to her about it. Maybe I should have but I just couldn't. I've never found anybody I could really talk to about it. I'd just as soon end it anyway, see? I don't know how you live. I just can't do it and feel like I fit, because I don't fit. I don't fit anywhere. I was a leader, believe it or not; everybody knew I was a leader. And it's true. I always had to be the best, had to run the fastest, farthest, and be there first. I even went to track just because of a dare. Wound up beating everybody in the state until I got to the state rallies. From then on everything's been the same, all of a sudden you just clam up inside, you're not the big kid or the joker anymore, the fun-loving guy."

After the interview I evaluated the case and came to the conclusion, as I wrote Mr. O'Connor, that "we have here a thirty-six-year-old white male, the product of a childhood that was practically designed to create a pathological character structure."

I went on:

Ray embarks upon a life characterized by episodes of primitive, cruel aggression. The episode with Mrs. Cantor in 1964 differs only in the extent of damage inflicted in the brutal murder of the farmer and his wife. In both instances we are dealing with senseless, sadistic, uncontrollable behavior. In both instances the brutality of the attack should not be confused with planned, goal-directed behavior. With Mrs. Cantor there was the element of unprovoked impulsiveness and the intensity of the viciousness with which she was attacked. The same elements are present in the behavior toward the couple he killed.

I am inclined to believe that the version indicating that Mr. Boxer merely stopped because his car was overheating and then entered the house is, in fact, the closest to the truth. The events then proceed unrelated to anything in reality. His victims do not resist him. He has no gain of any kind in torturing them or killing them. Nevertheless, he proceeds to inflict upon them the most cruel mental anguish imaginable, and tortures them physically—all this in the presence of their own child. Upon completion of these activities, he stops at the bar and has his usual drink, and behaves as if nothing happened. The cruel deeds which he himself perpetrated become reality only when they are announced on the radio and television. Only then does he become sick to his stomach.

The issue at hand is whether or not Ray suffers from a disease of the mind. It is my opinion that we are dealing here with a definite mental disorder which can be traced for many years in the history of this individual, which is well documented.

In the absence of psychosis at the time of an interview, an individual is regarded by some not to be mentally ill. Nevertheless, longitudinal examination of behavior frequently reveals disrupted functioning requiring some definite external intervention. Most frequently in these instances, criminal sanctions are imposed. From a psychiatric standpoint, there is no reason why long-term behavior (life history) should be less persuasive than short-term behavior (interview). There are, however, those who view disorders of personality to be mental illness, and this is, in fact, the current view of the American Psychiatric Association.

I said it was my opinion that Ray Boxer committed the homicides in question "as the result of a disease of the mind from which he was suffering and that he did lack the will power to control his behavior."

I added that in preparing the insanity defense, one had to keep in mind that one of the major obstacles prevailing is the general assumption on the part of professional and lay opinion that criminal behavior is in all instances rational and goal-directed. There is, furthermore, the erroneous assumption that the plea of insanity leads to a possible finding of innocence. The term "acquitted by virtue of insanity" is a misnomer, since those who are acquitted under the insanity plea do not go free but are subjected to commitment to a mental hospital. I said there was very little doubt in my mind that the public is better protected by having an individual committed to a mental institution than by having him sentenced to a jail term. The individual himself is usually also much better served in a psychiatric setting, particularly if he has long-term emotional problems.

Ray could not be set free. He would be a danger to society probably for as long as he lived. He had suffered severe emotional damage which occurred too early in life to be correctable. Many children grow up abandoned in large part by a mother, but Ray had also witnessed too many scenes of violence when he was a baby and a child. When parents, or parent surrogates, act violently in front of a child, that child is usually doomed to a life of violence too.

It is an all too familiar and tragic story, the future event of callous murder casting its bloody shadow years before. The "in cold blood" type of killer usually has the same kind of childhood, emotionally speaking. It was spelled out in the report of the Diagnostic Center in Missouri, dated July 3, 1962, when Ray was twenty-four years old, twelve years before he murdered the farmer and his wife.

Ray Boxer is a twenty-four-year-old white recidivist [repeater] who is the product of a home in which his parents

were separated when he was an infant. He was subsequently
raised in numerous communities by his mother and a succession of . . . stepfathers. He started stealing at an early age,
spent more than a year in the Oregon Boys' School, and is
currently beginning his third felony incarceration. He has
never held a job for any length of time, and his service
adjustment was extremely poor, resulting in an undesirable
discharge while he was serving a sentence. Boxer is unable to
give any explanation for his behavior and apparently simply
does things on impulse. He is a very intelligent youth who
apparently is very talented both musically and artistically. He
speaks of pursuing further instruction in these areas in the
hopes of eventually making one or another of them his career.
One has the feeling he will probably be in trouble again in the
future. He states he never has difficulty serving time and
always gets along very well. One has the feeling that possibly
he commits offenses in order to do time because it offers him
some dependency which he never had in his earlier life. It is
felt that he should be encouraged to pursue art and music as
much as possible while serving this sentence in the hope that
he can straighten himself out in the future.

One of Ray's records noted he was eligible for parole, but it
had been refused at his request. He became an artist while in
prison, studying ten to twelve hours a day. Possibly he felt that
prison authorities, though in a punitive way, were showing him a
kind of caring he never received, or that because they were
punitive they represented the kind of care he had been accustomed to as a child, which was better than no care at all. He said,
"I look at prison the same way as I do out here." Life in the
world of reality was a prison, he was saying.

The phrase "product of a home in which parents separated"
hides the torment a child endures as he grows up with parents
who cannot get along with each other, who fight and tear each
other apart psychologically, if not physically. It hides the endless
moments, hours, weeks, years of raw hate on which a child is
nurtured, a hate he feels directed at him.

Ray said to me in the interview, "I screamed help for the
last ten years." He had been screaming "help" all his life. "Right
from the start, I was by myself, I had nobody to help me," he
said. As a baby, then as a child, he felt lost, alone, without a
mother or father to depend on. Unless a child is able to feel

secure in his dependency on a mother, he can never break free of her; he will remain an angry, very dependent person, lonely, lost.

He told me, "I've been so lonely I wanted to die all my life." And "I don't fit. I don't fit anywhere." He said, "A day in solitary would crack me up," speaking of prison, where he always was well behaved. Solitary was too painful since he felt he had spent his life in solitary. He suffered deep depression. He said, "I get so damned depressed I want to crawl off and die, for no reason, just all of a sudden start bawling and feel sad, feel lonely." When he was happiest in his married life, he would "crawl off and start bawling" in the basement or hide in the garage. This is not the behavior of a man but a hurt child.

Such deep depression starts in childhood, possibly in the cradle. Ray's first impression of his father must have been that of a drunken, cruel man who tried to destroy Ray's mother. A baby will sense and absorb the mood of his parents even if he does not understand what is going on around him.

His mother said of his father, "I could take no more of his getting drunk and beating me, so when Ray was ten months old I left his father." This does not agree with Ray's story of his father's becoming crippled and then dying which may have been fantasy, a wish, in his emotionally crippled life.

We can only imagine how Ray felt when, as a baby, he saw his father stumbling around the room, cursing, smelling of whiskey, heard his mother plead, "Please, don't!" saw his father crash his fist into his mother's face, watched the blood streaming down her cheeks, heard her anguished cries. Ray must have lain in his crib terrified at the noise, the scene of violence.

Then stepfather after stepfather also drank, so Ray probably saw the same scene repeated as he grew older, watched his mother take beatings from the men who supposedly loved her. He no doubt wondered why his mother chose such cruel men but at the same time thought this must be the kind of man his mother wanted since she loved them. His image of man would be one of cruelty, drunkenness, violence. Violence can be exciting to a child. The presence of violence in a child's life may cause him to confuse danger and excitement all his life. His sexual and aggressive feelings never become separate, nor does he ever get a chance to know what tenderness is.

Ray's mother undoubtedly had little time or energy to give

to her baby the first years of his life, coping with such men as she chose as husbands. After his father disappeared, Ray saw a succession of seven stepfathers come and go as his mother either took him with her all over the country or left him with maternal or paternal grandparents, returning for him when it suited her.

We can imagine the look on the face of this bereft, angry little boy as his mother dumped him with his suitcase time and time again, leaving him alone. As she walked out of the grandparents' house, away from him, we can only guess at the grief and fury in his heart. A child wants to be with his mother at any cost. No one else can substitute for her. Ray felt rejected over and over as a little boy, and when we feel rejected we hate the one who rejects us and causes us so much deep pain.

Even the times he was with her and a new stepfather were unsettling, for it is emotionally disruptive even for a child who has happy parents to move from place to place, feeling he has no roots. Ray attended only one school for more than a year at a time. While staying with his father's parents, he completed eighth grade at the Hall of the Divine Child Catholic Military School in Monroe, Michigan. We might wonder why his grandparents at one point tried to keep his mother from taking him. Were they saying she was not fit to raise him? She had to kidnap him, he said, which must have been exciting, but then when she brought him back, unable to take care of him, he must have felt fiercely rejected.

He never learned tenderness or thoughtfulness. This is revealed in his words, "Everybody's out to do you in, hurt you in some way or use you." And "I hurt too easy. . . . Constantly people are hurting me."

He hurt others as he felt he had been hurt. One wonders, since he so often used a knife to attack others and to slit his own wrist, if he had heard his mother, in her misery with the successive men in her life, threaten to cut her wrists. Possibly she even made a suicide attempt somewhere along the way in such fashion.

He started stealing when a freshman in high school and never stopped. He said, "I committed so many burglaries I can't remember locations and what was taken." Burglary became a way of life. He recalled one time entering a house in Bethany, Missouri, in the dead of night and stealing a thirty-dollar wristwatch and a flashlight.

He was too crippled to grow up emotionally. He had an overwhelming need for his mother. He yearned for her desperately, went AWOL for her when in the Army, but he hated her just as desperately for deserting him when he needed her. During the Brevital interview, his hate emerged as his buried feelings pushed their way to the surface under the influence of drugs. His mother had been unable to give the minimal emotional nourishment a child needs to be emotionally healthy.

He said, "My mother and I never were really too close. . . . I could never figure Mom out." How could a child figure out a mother who, out of her own emotional disturbance, married eight times and left the child whenever she felt like it? Ray must have packed his own suitcase so many times, or had it packed for him, or seen his mother pack hers, that the sight of the packed suitcase in the Rogers home may have sent him into an uncontrollable rage (a suitcase appeared in his painting of the junkyard). We might raise the question whether, if Mrs. Rogers had not been pregnant and her suitcase packed and left in full view, the murders would have occurred. While he never saw his mother pregnant, because he was an only child, he would have fantasies that she might become pregnant and bear a rival, and he would want to kill the rival. He had a stepsister from his mother's fourth marriage. His mother also may have had miscarriages along the way, or abortions.

He told me, "I get along better with women than I do men. Men I don't trust worth a damn." And why should he, seeing brutal stepfathers come and go, snatching his mother from him? They were probably never loving toward him, for it is difficult to love another man's child if you are emotionally disturbed, and it is likely that his mother, disturbed as she was, would also pick as a husband an equally disturbed man.

His ambivalence toward his mother is seen in the tattoo on his arm. Love and hate combined. A beautiful rose and a dagger, his instrument of death. The tattoo once kept him from getting a job as a lifeguard. He had a scar in his left eyebrow and a one-inch scar on his upper lip, according to the record, but no indication of how he had gotten them.

His sexual life shows that fusion of violence and sexuality that appears so often in the criminal. To him sex was a violent act. In his own words, when his wife told him she didn't care for sex, he used sex "to get even." He was "mad" at her when he insisted on intercourse for several hours, which must have been very painful for her. He said of sex, "A lot of that was just hate." He raped his stepdaughter. He tried to stab one woman, assaulted another. He strangled a woman after asking her to take off her pantyhose and bare her body.

He believed he was sexually adequate, but the fact that he could have three to five orgasms and "still not feel tired or satisfied" means he was not getting real sexual satisfaction, which includes emotional pleasure as well as physical. He was incapable of tenderness or thoughtfulness toward a woman. How could he be tender or thoughtful, feeling broken, unmanly? When he got married, trying to take on the responsibility of an adult, he suffered intense migraine headaches, undoubtedly related to sexual conflicts, and started grinding his teeth in such unconscious rage that he had to go to a dentist.

He "broke into" filling stations, bars, houses. He described his bodily sensations in the farmhouse as "getting all keyed up" while in the closet and "worked up" as he roamed the house looking for money, after he had tied up the man and woman. Following the murders, he said, "My mind was ringing," and "My heartbeat was going ninety miles an hour," sensations that occur after the act of sex.

We might ask why he murdered at this particular time in his life. It is obvious from his past record that he had been building up to murder—first small burglaries, then the theft of cars, grand larceny, then the threatened stabbing of a woman, then assault on a woman, then the murder of a man and woman. Why did he not kill the little girl? Perhaps in his mind the child represented himself, the only child, a child now left without a mother or father, as he believed he had been.

This was also a time he felt abandoned once again by his family. He had not seen his mother in fourteen years; she had no doubt given him up completely after his terms in prison, wanting nothing more to do with him. His wife had cancer and might be dying and had given him up; he had raped his stepdaughter. He felt he wasn't a man; he had lost his job, was unable to provide for his family, had deserted them. His act of desertion would revive memories of all the early desertions by his mother.

When he insisted that he did not know why he had killed, saying, "I can't see myself doing it," he was telling the truth in that consciously he really did not know—one measure of the dissociative state.

He said, "I didn't have any hate for those people," referring to the farmer and his pregnant wife, and at the moment he said this, for the first and only time, tears came to his eyes, as he felt guilt. He did not hate the farmer and his wife. How could he? He did not even know them. But the emotions aroused within him at seeing them together in a farmhouse stirred memories of seeing his mother with a man, a number of men who had treated him cruelly. He was again part of a trio, but as an outcast, a stranger who had just wandered in, belonging to nobody. He once again felt the rejection, and the hurt and hatred he had borne over the years exploded as, out of work, given up by a wife, he could stand no more of his suppressed fury.

When he tied up and murdered the farmer, he was in fantasy murdering his father and all his stepfathers. When he murdered the farmer's wife, he was murdering his mother, who had so often made him feel the outcast. He was not consciously aware of his hatred for his mother; all he experienced was what he called "a keyed-up feeling" as he zeroed in for the kill, finally able to exact his revenge.

Because of the cruelties inflicted on him, sometimes knowingly, sometimes unknowingly, by those who cared for him as a child, Ray, in his desire for revenge, could not differentiate between the guilty and the innocent. His fantasies of revenge were so strong that they overpowered all reality. What was done unto him as a child, he did unto others as an adult.

3

"I Wondered Why I Did It"

James Turner went to work with a hangover at 6 A.M. on January 18, 1969. His car had broken down, so his father, promising he would fix the car that morning, drove his twenty-two-year-old son to the factory a few miles from Middletown, Michigan, where they lived. James had been staying with his parents for three weeks.

That morning he felt groggy, as though still half asleep. During the 9 A.M. break, he sat in a friend's car, drinking a beer, hoping it would clear his mind. He thought of his car breaking down, all the bills he hadn't paid, and his pregnant wife, Jessica, who was starting proceedings for a divorce after only nine months of marriage. Even his girl friend Alice had said she was through with him. And his father and mother had quarreled violently the week before. His father had told his mother to get out of the house, that he wanted a divorce. James felt so depressed that he thought he had to either get away from Middletown or kill himself.

He knew one thing—he couldn't stand the job any longer, fitting bolts into car engines on an endless assembly line. Nor could he bear getting up every day at 5 A.M., usually with a hangover. So, after he finished the beer, he went over to the foreman and said, "I'm quitting."

"You can leave right now," said the foreman.

James walked out of the factory and headed for the highway, where he hitched a ride back to Middletown. There he went into a local bar and ordered a beer. A few minutes later his older brother Tony and Tony's friend Larry came in. Seeing him, they sat down and joined him in a beer.

"Why aren't you at work?" Tony asked. He was on his own, part owner of a local garage, the garage where his father had taken the car to be fixed.

"I quit," James said. "It's a lousy job."

"That's a dumb thing to do," his brother said. "You owe a lot of money. You have to support your wife, especially since she's expecting a baby. You haven't paid off your car. And Mom and Dad expect you to pay them while you're living there."

"Fifteen dollars a week," James said bitterly. They had charged Tony and his older sister only ten dollars a week when they had lived at home.

"You haven't even paid for the three weeks you've been there," said Tony. "That's a helluva way to treat them."

"I guess you're right," James said. He sighed. "Jessica expects too much. Don't ever get married, Tony. You'll only get hurt."

Each of them ordered a second beer. Then Tony and Larry got up to leave. James asked, "Could Larry give me a lift home? He goes right past the house."

"Sure, kid," said Larry.

On the short drive to his parents' house James said to Larry, "I mean it. Don't get married. Women hurt you. Even my girl friend's given me the gate."

"Why?" Larry asked.

"She says I drink too much." He had been drinking beer since seventh grade. What was wrong with drinking? His father drank a lot, and so did his brother.

"Cheer up," said Larry. "You've just got a hangover."

"No one wants me," he said. Then, in a very depressed voice, "And I don't care what happens. I don't want to live."

"Buck up, kid," said Larry. "You can find an easier job

where you don't have to get up before the chickens. And you'll find another gal you like. There's plenty of 'em.'' He chuckled. ''I know.''

Larry parked for a few minutes in front of James's house, trying to cheer him up. He finally said, ''I gotta go. Take it easy, kid.''

It was then about noon. James walked slowly across the small front lawn toward the two-story red brick house in which he had grown up. The house was quiet; only his mother was home. He went to the refrigerator, which was usually filled with beer for his father. He took out a can, opened it, and carried it upstairs to his room, which had remained empty the nine months he had been living with his wife and the months he had lived in his own apartment, which he had had to give up because he fell behind on the rent.

His mother came into his room. She was wearing a red print dress and high-heeled shoes. She looked very pretty, her hair, blond like his, all fluffed out. She stared at him in surprise and said, ''What are you doing home?''

''I quit my job,'' he said.

''That's not a very good way to pay your bills,'' she said reprovingly.

He could not reply; he felt utter defeat as she said this, as though she were reminding him once again of his inadequacy, of all the failures in his life. It all seemed too much; he was not going to make it, would never be able to stand on his own. He lifted the beer can to his mouth.

She went downstairs to the living room. After a few swallows, he put the can of beer on the bureau and followed her down.

''Where're you going, all dressed up?'' he asked.

''Grandma's coming over and we're going shopping,'' she said. She picked up a magazine and sat down on the overstuffed brown sofa.

At that moment he had the strange impulse to kill his mother. Then he thought of killing himself. He recalled the shotgun his father used to hunt deer. It was kept in the basement.

He left his mother and went down to the basement. He took the shotgun off the wall and loaded it. He wondered whether to kill his mother or himself. He could not do away with himself with a shotgun. Pills, maybe, but not with a gun. He laid the gun down on an old wooden table.

He walked upstairs to his room and finished the beer. He kept thinking of his mother sitting in the living room waiting for her mother. He went back to the basement. He seized the shotgun, walked up the steps to the kitchen and into the living room.

He looked at his mother for a moment. He raised the gun, pointed it at her, pulled the trigger. The shot hit her in the face. She gave him a look of pain and terror, as though asking why. He couldn't stand the look. He shot her again, this time in the stomach. She crumpled over in the chair, lost consciousness.

He left her slumped in the chair. He walked to the refrigerator, took out another can of beer, and went up to his room to drink it. He thought his dad might be coming home soon with the fixed car, so he'd better leave the house. But first he wanted to call his wife, tell her he was going to kill himself, and ask if she would see him for one last time. Her line was busy. So instead he wrote a note to his girl friend, Alice, saying he had just killed his mother and that he loved her, Alice. He put the letter in his pocket. Then he went to the basement for the extra shells for the gun, thinking he might use it to kill himself.

He thought that before he left he had better hide his mother so no one would find her. He couldn't lift her, so he dragged her upstairs, intending to put her body into her bedroom closet. As he passed her bed, he had the sudden urge to have intercourse with her. He lifted her onto the bed, pulled up her dress and pulled down her underpants. He unbuttoned her blouse. She was wearing a full-length slip. He walked down to the kitchen, got a knife, walked upstairs again, and cut the straps of the slip.

Then he went into his room and took off all his clothes. He returned to his mother. He spread her legs, then inserted his fingers into her vagina and spread it apart, too, as he looked into it.

He got on his knees between her legs, bent over, and sucked her breasts. Then he took his penis and rubbed it against her vagina. He could not get an erection. He gave up trying after a few minutes, returned to his room, put on his clothes.

He went back to his mother's room. He thought her closet

would be too small to hide her body, so he started to drag her across the hall to his brother's bedroom, where there was a larger closet. Blood had started to flow from the gunshot wounds and was leaving a trail. He thought there really wasn't any sense in trying to hide her; he might as well leave her on the floor. Her face still had the tormented, pained expression of the moment he shot her, so he covered her face with one of his sweatshirts.

He opened her purse and took out ten dollars. He went to the refrigerator and gathered up the remaining six bottles of beer, putting them into a shopping bag along with a bottle of rye his father kept on a kitchen shelf. Taking the shopping bag and the shotgun, he left the house and climbed into his parents' car, which was parked in the driveway.

He was planning to leave the house and town and state forever, but decided first to stock up on beer. He stopped at a local delicatessen, where he bought two dozen cans. Then he decided to drive to Kalamazoo to see Alice, even though she had told him she didn't want to see him anymore. He thought he might persuade her to have sex one last time; if she refused, he might rape her, or even kill her and then have intercourse. He thought of his mother and how he had failed to get an erection after she was dead. The shotgun by his side smelled after being fired twice, and reminded him too much of his dead mother, so he threw it out of the car as he drove along.

He arrived at the apartment where Alice lived and rang the bell. She opened the door, looked at him in surprise, and asked, "Why aren't you at work?"

"I quit my job," he said. "Can I come in?"

"Just for a minute," she said. "I have to go to work." She waited on tables at a diner, afternoons and evenings.

He told her, "I've done something terrible. I probably won't ever see you again."

"What did you do?" she asked.

"I can't tell you," he said. "But it's all here." He pulled from his pocket the letter he had written her.

"Let me see it," she said.

"No," he said, changing his mind about giving the letter to her. He didn't want her to learn what he had done while he was with her. "I'll mail it to you."

"I really must go to work," she said. "I don't want to lose my job."

He drove away, not knowing where to head but thinking he might go south. He turned on the radio. First there was music. Then there was a news broadcast announcing that his mother's body had been found in the house. He heard his name mentioned, then that the police were searching for him and his parents' car. They had put up roadblocks, the announcer said.

He thought now that he had to kill himself before he could be picked up. He no longer had the gun, but he could take an overdose of pills. He stopped at a drug store. He did not have enough money left to buy sleeping pills, so he bought a bottle of aspirin.

While driving, he chewed and swallowed eight aspirin. He didn't know how many it would take to kill him but figured he could get the whole bottle down by night, and then he would be dead.

Suddenly he saw a police car approaching from the opposite direction. The car slowed down as it came directly opposite him. The cop looked suspiciously at him and the car.

The police car swerved and made a U-turn. It started to overtake him.

He pulled to the side of the road and waited.

✧✧✧✧✧✧✧

James Turner was charged with the first degree murder of his mother. I was asked by his attorney, Robert H. Warner, of Warner, Hart & Morgan, who had been appointed by the court to represent James, to testify in court as to his sanity at the time of the crime.

Mr. Warner sent me the report of Dr. Alexander P. Dukay, superintendent of Ypsilanti State Hospital and clinical associate professor of psychiatry at the University of Michigan, who was a good friend of mine. He had examined James to determine his mental condition at the time he killed his mother. Dr. Dukay's evaluation was based on James's personal history, obtained during an interview, as well as from a direct psychiatric examination; from written material made available by the prosecuting attorney;

and from a verbal report of the "turnkey" at the Eaton County
Jail, where James was being held.

From Dr. Dukay's report I learned that James was the
youngest of three children; he had an older sister and brother. His
father, forty years old, worked for an electric power company.
The family was Protestant.

James said of his father: "He liked to keep his bills up.
There were no arguments in the marriage. He is okay. I take after
my dad. He is five feet eleven, weighs approximately 190 pounds.
I currently weigh about 175, but previously I had a big stomach
from drinking and was much heavier."

He said of his mother: "She was nice. She always got along
with everybody. Dad was the boss. They would not go against
one another. She did not care to go out; it was up to Dad. Dad
made the decisions. They did get along well. There was nothing
wrong about that relationship. No arguments. Everything was just
fine. I always got the impression they favored my brother and
sister more. They made her pay ten dollars when she was staying
home, my brother had to pay ten dollars. I had to pay fifteen
dollars, however. I felt closer to my mother but don't remember
much about it. I do recall when I was young, I cannot tell you
exactly how old, my mother was standing at the window. I was on
my hands and knees and slid up behind her and looked up her
dress."

Of his childhood: "I don't remember much about my childhood. I guess it was average. I can't remember anything happy,
nothing outstanding. The only thing I remember was that Dad
slapped my sister. I felt very bad about that, but can't remember
much. I was in trouble when I was sixteen. My dad agreed to put
me in a detention home to teach me a lesson. That's about all that
I remember about my childhood.

"The first things that I actually remember is when I started
kindergarten or first grade. We all had to get up on the first day in
school and give our names. I was shy. I cried. My brother took
me home. He was very mad about it. I was always scared on the
first day of school; otherwise I was all right."

Of his school days: "When I was in country school in the
elementary grades, we went out to smoke cigarettes. We told this
one girl to let us see her breasts. We unbuttoned her blouse, but

she fought us, so we left her alone. I remember this country schoolteacher. We always wanted to have intercourse with her. We looked down her neck to look at her breasts. I remember walking home with this girl when we were going to the country school. I asked her whether or not she knew what 'fuck' means. I laid on top of her. She did not like it. I remember this girl in high school when I was fifteen years old. We got to the state when I rubbed my penis against her, usually in the car or when she was babysitting. We had intercourse, and we carried this on for about a year and a half."

Of his marriage: "Then I started to go with my wife. She never went out with boys before. I was already drinking whiskey and I gave her some, and we had sex. I got married because most guys get married. I guess it was just convenient to have sex anytime. I think I loved her, but I did not plan to spend my life with her. I just could not stay with one girl. I would get drunk and argue with her. I would get mad and hit her. She caught me with this other girl. I was running around. My wife caught me with her in the car; she started to open the door, and I tried to close it. Her hand got caught between the door and the frame of the car and I started up the car and dragged her until a stop sign. She said I did this on purpose, that I wanted to kill the baby. This happened on or about May 20, 1968. We had lived just nine months together then. I was staying in an apartment and continued to go with this girl friend of mine, but wanted to have my wife stop the divorce and have her come back to me. She always thought lots more about her own folks than me. She agreed to come together again after I would be in a better financial situation. I was drinking quite a bit and this girl did not like it, so she called me up just one week before all this happened [the murder of his mother] and told me she did not want to do anything with me."

The report by Dr. Dukay continued:

School: "I think I liked it. I always went out with my cousin. I had a good time. The main reason I liked school was to go with the girls. I had a grade of C-minus, but graduated from high school in 1965. I liked the choir. That was my favorite. I got into trouble the first semester. They kicked me out. I broke in this house. I was running around with this older man, drinking quite a bit. I broke in to get some money to buy whiskey, to show off. I knew that the farmers where I used to work keep their money in a pot in the kitchen. I walked in the house, using a white stocking cap. I set the haystack on fire. I really did not want to burn down the barn. I just wanted the man out of the kitchen. This was when I was sixteen, sometime in October 1963. I took the money, but they caught me a day or two after. The police came to my house. They found my brother's white stocking cap, but mine was gone, so I confessed it. That was the time when I was in the detention home. After I came home everyone was so nice to me. Mother wanted to fix me breakfast. Nobody said anything. They were real nice. They seemed to be nice about it.''

Occupation: "During the last year of school I started to wash dishes. Went to a small factory in Nashville, a plywood factory. Worked three or four months, then I went to Oldsmobile in Lansing. Stayed just a year, did not like the long drive. Then I worked in Middleville until my wife left me. My cousin talked me into taking a job in Detroit. My dad told me, too, that I could not stay home if I did not pay up. I worked in Detroit for three months, but we were just messing around, drinking. In the apartment and in the car. When I was drunk occasionally I would come back to Middletown, go back to my wife, stay with her, have intercourse with her; then my cousin and me came back to Middletown to hang drywall. We did a job, got paid, and then we would drink. We drank as we earned the money. We ran out of contractors who would hire us. Then I got a job outside of Middletown, August 1968, as a lathe man, making houses. I worked last on January 18, 1969 [at the factory]."

Alcohol: "Started drinking in junior high, seventh or eighth grade. Was running around with my cousin, was running around with these older men. Looking always for older men to buy me a drink. Would get mad and depressed if I would not find anyone. After I got twenty-one I just drank as much money as I had. Drink and ride around by myself. I drank mostly beer. I just drank to feel relaxed. I drank gin and tonic for a while. When I was drinking I was just roaming around. Cry on my cousin's shoulder. I went out with this married woman Friday night. Her husband knew my cousin. I was out there at the trailer park. We were drinking. She wanted to go out with me. I would ask him [her husband] if I could take his wife out. He said yes, so he could get rid of her, so he could do what he wanted. She started to talk about getting married. She started a divorce. I could not see how to get married with three kids. She got pregnant by me. No, I don't know anything about her. It doesn't bother me."

Cousin: "He is my mother's sister's boy. Same age. Felt closest to him. We had in common drink. He was the only child. The parents would let him do much more stuff. Both parents were working, he could do what he wanted to. He was wild. I could not see him settling down with one girl. He got married after I came in here [the jail]."

Health: Tonsillectomy when a child. Digestion—no problems. Appetite—good. Sleeps soundly. Very seldom dreams.

Personality: "I never had any hobbies. Did not participate in games. Played with trucks. No interests whatsoever. I did go to the Bible school when we were in the country. My parents do not attend church. My sister belongs to the Protestant church. I always thought that people were talking behind my back. I was always self-conscious around people, wondering whether they liked me. When I came back from Detroit, people wondered whether my cousin and I were homosexuals. We were kissing in the soda fountain when my wife was driving by just to make her think so. I had a homosexual experience three, four years ago. Met this guy through my cousin. He took my pants down. Started to suck it. Did not get hard. I started touching him. He laid on top of me. Never enjoyed it."

Present difficulty: "Actually started when I got behind in my bills. I was not making much money in the factory. I moved back home, gave money to my dad. My car broke down again. I drank Friday night again. My father woke me up so I would go to work. I just felt funny. Did not sleep enough, or maybe too much drinking. All these things came back to me: my car breaking down, my wife not wanting me, the girl friend not wanting me, all these bills. I thought about killing myself. . . ."

Questioned as to why he murdered his mother, he said, "I don't have any reason why I did it. I think I should be committed. I need help for my mind."

Dr. Dukay described James as "well developed, well nourished, well groomed, of medium complexion, dressed in jail overalls, clean-shaven, neat and clean in his appearance. He is cooperative in the interview and volunteers information readily. He smokes a cigarette just about every fifteen minutes during the interview, sits most of the time rigidly in the chair, opposite the examiner, with downcast eyes. His facial expression is most often expressionless; however, occasionally he laughs inappropriately. There is no overt expression of anxiety, and he appears unconcerned, detached, and most often without any emotional expression. He is relevant and coherent in his speech, and his reaction time is average without any evidence of psychomotor hyperactivity or retardation. His affect [emotion] is shallow, most often fixed, with occasional change manifested by inappropriate laughter. He expresses great amount of ambivalence toward women. His thought processes are characterized by paucity of ideas, concrete and autistic [highly personal] thinking, and a splitting off of the emotional feelings from his thought processes. His consciousness is clear. He is oriented as to time, place and person. His recent and past memory are unimpaired. School and general knowledge are average. He is of average intelligence. He lacks insight into his problems, and his judgment is poor.''

Dr. Dukay diagnosed James as a man with alcohol addiction, an antisocial personality, a schizoid personality, suffering from hysterical neurosis. He said James showed a simple type of schizophrenia, based on the disturbance of his emotions, mood, ambivalence, and thought processes which were characterized by autistic and concrete thinking.

I interviewed James on April 20, 1969, at the Charlotte County Jail. After the interview I asked him to write me in his own words about his childhood, what happened the day he shot his mother, and his recent dreams. The interview and his letter covered the same subjects, so I reprint the letter which I received on April 28, 1969, written in a neat though childish handwriting in pencil on both sides of blue-lined notebook paper:

Dear Mr. Tanay:
    This is an answer to your request of me writing about my childhood and the shooting of my mother. First the shooting. Jan. 18, 1969.
    I came home around 4 A.M. from drinking the night before. I had to go work at 6 A.M. but my car had broke down so I didn't think I had a way. My dad woke me up and said he

would take me. So, I got dressed, cleaned up and had breakfast (none of which I can remember doing).

I gave the keys to my car to my dad as he was going to
fix it while I was at work.

I can't remember much that happened at work. First the
fact that everything seemed fussy [fuzzy], like I was still half
asleep. I went out at break time (9 A.M.) with a buddy, to his
car to have a beer hoping this would straighten my mind out.
It didn't seem to help so we went back to work.

I was so depressed by my car breaking down all the
time and I was far behind on all my bills that I just decided to
quit my job. I was thinking of either just traveling or of killing
myself.

So, I quit and hitchhiked to town [Middletown] and went
to a bar. I was there for about fifteen minutes and my brother
Tony and a friend, Larry, came in. Tony wanted to know
why I wasn't working and I told him. He talked about my
folks trying to help me with my bills and everything, and that
this wasn't a very good way to treat them. I agreed, but it
seemed like I just had to do it.

Then I started telling him never to get married because
he would just get hurt. (My wife, Jessica, was giving me a
divorce.)

We was at the bar about half, three quarters of a hour
and they had to leave. I asked if Larry could take me home.
On the way out I was talking about Jessica hurting me and
also a girl I had been going with, Alice. She had told me last
week that she didn't want to see me any more because of my
drinking. Also, I mentioned me being behind on my bills and
that I just didn't care any more of what happened.

We sat in my folks' driveway for a while and finally he
had to leave so I went into the house. I went right to my room
and was drinking a beer that I had. My mother came in and
asked what I was doing. I told her I had quit my job and she
said I couldn't get my bills paid that way and went back into
the living room and sat down.

I asked her if she was going any place as she was
dressed up. She said she was going shopping with my
grandma shortly. I think I can remember thinking about
shooting her then, but I don't know.

I then called my foreman at work and told him my
brother would pick my last check up.

Then I went down in the basement as that's where the

shotgun was. I loaded it and just stood there wondering what to do. I think I was thinking about killing myself but couldn't do it with a shotgun. I put the gun down and went back up to my room and finished the beer that I had. All this time my mother was still sitting in the living room.

I finished the beer and went back down in the basement. I then thought of shooting my mother, but I couldn't understand why. I figured if I was going to do it I would have to hurry as my mother would be leaving soon or my dad would come home from fixing my car. So I just walked upstairs and shot her.

She kinda jumped and looked at me with the expression of pain, terror, wondering what happened and why I was doing it. I'll never forget the way she looked. So, I just shot her again. I turned my head and wondered why I did it. I went to the refrigerator and got a beer and went in my room. Then I thought of my dad coming home so I went back downstairs and got the shells to reload the gun. I was up in my room and decided I better leave before anyone came.

I then thought of calling my wife as I was going to kill myself and I wanted to see her for the last time. The line was busy, so I thought of writing my girl friend Alice, as I would be seeing her again. I wrote her and told her I had just killed my mother and that I loved her.

Then I thought of hiding my mother so no one would find her. I thought of her bedroom closet so I went and dragged her in her room. Then I thought of having intercourse with her. So I pulled her dress up and pulled her [panties] down. I unbuttoned her blouse and seen she had a full slip on so I went to the kitchen and got a knife and cut the straps. I went into my room and took my clothes off and went back to her room. I spread her legs apart and spread her vagina apart and looked at it. I was on my knees between her legs and bent over and sucked her breast. Then I took my penis and rubbed it against her vagina. It wouldn't get hard so I figured I could never do it. So I got up and went back to my room and got dressed.

I went back to her room and figured her closet was too small so I dragged her across to my brother's bedroom. She had started to bleed then and left a trail so I figured there wasn't any sense to hide her. So I just left her lying there with a sweatshirt over her face. I had covered her face in her bedroom as I couldn't stand to see her face. One of the shots had hit her face.

Then I thought of getting some more beer, but didn't have any money. I went through the house and found some in my mother's purse. I got all the beer and liquor in the house and put it in a sack. I got the letter I had wrote to Alice and put some shells in my pocket, got the gun and drove off with my folks' car.

I wanted to buy some more beer so I went straight to a store in the neighborhood. That was in the direction of Kalamazoo where Alice lived so after I got the beer I figured I would drive down to see her. I started thinking of having intercourse with her, but figured she wouldn't let me since she didn't want anything to do with me. I thought of raping her or killing her to do it, but remembered my mother and didn't think I could do it. I got down there and went inside. She was going to leave to go to work. We talked for a while and I told her I did something terrible and probably wouldn't see her again. She wanted to know what I did but I wouldn't tell her. She got the letter I had wrote to her, but I took it back as I didn't want her to find out what I did while I was there.

She said she had to go so I left. I really didn't know where I was going. I had the radio on in the car and heard Kalamazoo had roadblocks up looking for me. Then I thought I had to kill myself before they picked me up. I didn't have the gun anymore as the smell of it just being fired reminded me of what I had done so I had thrown it alongside the road on the way to Kalamazoo.

I thought of taking some pills so I stopped at a store and bought some aspirins. I started driving again and took the aspirins. I seen a cop car coming toward me and then turn around so I just pulled over to the side and waited for him. He came and took me to the station. I guess that's about all.

I don't know why I killed her, just that I couldn't think very good that day. My mind would keep jumping to one thing and then another. As I said before, I felt like I was still half asleep.

I also can't remember when I first thought of killing my mother. Sometimes I think it was while I was at work. Either that or after I had gotten home. And I can't remember ever wanting to have intercourse with her.

James also related several dreams.

I've had some dreams since I've been in jail. I can't remember all of them, but I'll try.

In one I was with three creatures. A Frankenstein, a lion and some other kind. I was with them all the time.

Another, I was sleeping and woke up and people were standing around me with real ugly faces. I seen a movie like that once.

Another, my brother was to execute a man. Him and other people was on a platform. He just had a blank face, didn't seem to know what was going on. A man was on his knees with his hands tied behind his back. Someone gave my brother a gun and he shot the man on his knees in the back of the head. He didn't die, so he shot him again and then realized what he did. Then, he just looked around and started to run.

Other dreams I can remember when I was a kid was being chased by a dragon, fire and all.

Another, I was sleeping and I woke up and my dad had a tub of bricks and poured them on me.

Another, I was in a high building, standing with my back toward a window. Someone shot me in the stomach and I fell out the window. I woke up before I hit the ground.

Another, a friend of mine was a sheriff deputy. He was chasing my wife trying to rape her. My wife and I was in a shack and the deputy was trying to get in. I had a shotgun and just as I was closing the barrel after loading it, he got in and shot me. I woke up before the shell hit me.

Now, I'll just skip around on my childhood and put down what I can remember.

I have tried to rape several girls, but I always reach my climax before I actually raped them. I would get on top of them and touch and kiss their breast and that was all. I always told them I was sorry afterwards and made them feel sorry for me so they never told anyone.

After my wife started the divorce, I stayed at the apartment we had been living in. It was in town and girls would walk by on their way home from school. I would watch for them and when they came I would stand in front of the window without anything on. I guess I just wanted them to see me.

I went out on my wife quite a bit. I usually would ride around town drinking and pick up someone.

Sometimes, there would be months that would go by that I wouldn't have intercourse with my wife. I guess I didn't want to give her the satisfaction of knowing I wanted her. Sometimes, I would go in the bathroom and masturbate instead of having her.

I use to hit her quite a lot, before and after we were married. We would be arguing and I would tell her if she didn't stop I would hit her. She wouldn't stop, so I would slap her.

You mentioned me being afraid of her. I thought about it, and I guess I am. She could hurt my feelings and I don't like to be hurt. That's the only reason I can think of.

We never got along very good. We always argued and usually we wouldn't be together. And she would get mad and go back to her folks. Sometimes I wanted this so I could go out. I think we lived together about seven months out of the nine that we were married. I think the only reason I got married was because all my buddies was.

I have been with one homosexual. I never thought of being with one and didn't enjoy myself when I was. We was in the country drinking and we got out and laid on the grass. He started touching me, but it wouldn't get hard. Finally, he started to suck it and was laying beside me the opposite way. I didn't know what to do, so I just started to touch him. He asked me if he could lay on top of me and did. He reached his climax and that's all.

My cousin and I would be riding around town drinking and if anyone looked at us, we would pretend we were kissing. Just to make them stare I guess. They did!

When my brother and I was real young we use to take turns "milking" each other. One would get on his hands and knees and the other would "milk" his penis. Why, I don't know.

Also, when we were young, we were masturbating in bed one morning. I looked up and my mother was watching us. She just told us to get dressed.

When I was real young, my mother was standing in front of a window. I got on my back and shimmied to her and looked up her dress. She didn't see me.

My family used to go on camping trips. One night I was

sleeping next to my sister and I reached over and unzipped her sleeping bag. I was feeling her breast and she woke up. She just told me I better go to sleep.

When my sister and brother finished school and got a job, they had to pay my folks ten dollars a week to stay there. I never could see paying to live in my own home. Anyway, when I got a job, I had to pay fifteen dollars to stay there. I guess I've always held it against them for that (my folks).

I don't think we was a very close family. Or I wasn't. I always got in trouble and arguments. I never talked with them very much.

I always felt sorry for my mother when all of us kids moved from home (I was kicked out). My dad has to work nights sometime and usually when it's real stormy. She had to stay there by herself most of the time.

I can remember my folks only arguing twice when I was around. Once, when I was real young. The other was a week before I shot her. They were sitting at the table after eating and she was trying to explain something to him. He had been drinking most of the day and I guess didn't care what she said. Finally, he told her to pack her clothes and get out. She just went in her bedroom.

He came in my bedroom and we started talking about my bills. He mentioned that they might get a divorce. I guess I was shocked to hear it. I just wanted to get out of there so I went out drinking.

You asked if I had ever blacked out. One night my cousin and I was drinking wine. We was staying in Detroit working last summer. I was beginning to drink quite a lot of wine down there. We had drank about three bottles apiece and decided to drive to Middletown. We was going quite fast and he was driving. He came up to our exit and he slammed on the brakes. When I woke up we were on the exit the wrong way, half out in the lane of traffic. I guess he blacked out too, and neither one of us knows what happened. There wasn't any skid marks and the car wasn't damaged. I guess it was just shock, I don't know.

That's about all I can remember of my childhood. I know I was always self-conscious. I always thought people were looking at me. Over here, I can talk with other inmates. But, when we're out of our cells so they can see me, I hardly say anything. I always drank quite a lot before I could do anything. I guess for courage. Also, I didn't really care about anything when I was drunk. I hate to be alone, but was happy if I had some beer.

I guess that's about all. I hope I can hurry and get some help. If you can do anything to get it speeded up, I would appreciate it.

※※※※※※※

After the interview and after receiving the letter, I wrote Mr. Warner my evaluation. I said that James had related all the tragic events "without any expression of feeling, but with considerable free-floating anxiety." I added, "His emotional responses show typical flatness of affect, characteristic of individuals who suffer from a schizophrenic illness. He described insignificant events in the same manner that he described shooting his mother or attempting to have sexual relations with her after her death."

I said I thought "his relationship with his wife is of great significance. He separated from her in May 1968. It appears that he has never had a warm and close relationship with her. He states that he married her simply because 'all of my buddies were married.' He feels that he was not a good husband to her. He was not interested in having sexual relations with her and would frequently masturbate in the bathroom instead of having intercourse with her. It was of great importance to him that she was a virgin; in fact, he would always be interested to know if any woman he associated with was a virgin. This issue holds great significance for him. He defined being a virgin as 'meaning no one had her before.' His relationship with his wife became much worse when he discovered that she was pregnant. This was an idea which was very disturbing to him. He describes his wife as a very nice person and a very good wife."

I also wrote: "Throughout his childhood, Mr. Turner appears to have been a rather remote and distant youngster. He did not relate well to any member of the family, although he describes his mother as a good and loving provider, not too strict. He seems to have had no friends and describes himself as a self-conscious youngster and a lonely adolescent. The only time he felt some relief was when he was drinking beer. In fact, he has been drinking increasingly more and more to overcome his tormenting feelings of uncontrollable anxiety. In spite of these difficulties, he was able to complete high school. He did not enter the military service because of the burglary charge which occurred when he was sixteen years old. This episode is described as an attempt to get some money from the farmer for whom he was working. To divert the farmer from the house, Mr. Turner set fire to a haystack.

"Mr. Turner states that he has always had problems in relations with women. On a number of occasions in his life he has forced his attentions on various unwilling females, but usually would get an ejaculation before introducing his penis into the vagina and then would become very guilt-ridden and sorry, so that these women would feel sorry for him and never pressed any charges.

"I would like to call your attention to the Barry County sheriff's report where the father describes James as a 'strange, moody boy who would go for weeks without talking to anyone, had been in trouble with police prior to this incident.' " I pointed out that Tony's friend Larry had made a statement to the police in which he described James as "very upset, nervous and tense, mixed up."

I also said, "It is interesting to note that the police report indicates that Mr. Turner behaved in a manner as if he expected to be apprehended. The police officer did not even have to put on his blue lights or siren before Mr. Turner pulled to the side of the road."

In my summary and conclusions, I stated: "We have here an individual who at the time of this examination shows signs and symptoms of a psychotic illness manifested by flat affect, remoteness and vagueness. Furthermore, there is history of having been withdrawn, 'moody and strange,' in the past. There is history of explosive sexual acting out, inability to form any close relationships. In brief, the patient has a typical schizoid pattern. The act itself was committed after a period of intense inner turmoil. The patient describes being driven to commit this dreadful act upon his mother, without any kind of provocation or emotional interaction. The inappropriateness of the act, and the description of the patient, clearly conveys the psychotic, consciously not motivated act. The patient describes performing actions as if he had to do it on the command of someone else. His description conveys clearly the depersonalization seen in schizophrenic homicide. The same thing applies to his sexual activities upon the body of his deceased mother. Once again, it is as if someone else were doing it.

"It is my opinion that the acute state of the illness in this man began as long ago as a few months prior to the act. In fact, the pregnancy of his wife seems to have been an intolerable threat to him. The psychodynamics of these reactions to pregnancy, as well as his inability to tolerate marriage, had to do with his deep-seated Oedipal complex, which I can elaborate upon once I am presenting this fully during direct examination. At this point, it suffices to say that in my opinion this act was committed by a man who was psychotic for some time prior to the commitment of this act, and certainly suffered from a severe and acute psychotic break that particular day. The act occurred, in my opinion, as the result of an irresistible impulse; there was no conscious intention on the part of Mr. Turner to perform the act, even though he consciously perceived the impulse to do so, but he was powerless to control it."

Mr. Warner, in another letter to me, had written that James, "without any apparent explanation or provocation whatever, picked up his twelve-gauge Mosberg Magnum Pump shotgun and proceeded up the stairs and shot his mother twice. . . . His only explanation for this action is that he wanted to kill himself and knew that he should 'do something bad' in order to justify his contemplated suicide." He freely admitted molesting his mother sexually "because it seemed the logical thing to do." Mr. Warner also said that James had broken down and cried several times, saying he was depressed and had to leave town. He indicated also that he "loved" his parents very much, that they "meant well" and he knew they were trying to help him. But his brother had said that in the past James had shown some bitterness toward his parents.

The trial took place in Middletown. I testified in court, evaluating James Turner much as I had done in the letter to his attorney. The psychiatrist for the prosecution was Dr. Alex Dukay, who, as I said, was an old friend of mine, for we had lived in the same building when I worked at Ypsilanti State Hospital. Alex was a debonair Hungarian, admired by his colleagues and considered charming by the ladies. I told Mr. Warner, the attorney, that we had nothing to fear, because Alex would be fair and honest; he was a devoted father and an exemplary husband. I would never have believed that Alex would one day be in a position similar to that of James Turner; just a few years later, Alex killed his wife, his beloved twelve-year-old daughter, his dog, and then himself.

At the trial, James Turner was acquitted by virtue of insanity and sent to Kalamazoo State Hospital on August 7, 1969. In May 1974 his attorneys asked me to go to Battle Creek to testify in the Probate Court at a hearing on the discharge of Turner. The attorneys met me at the airport and seemed rather gloomy about the prospects because the hearing was before a judge they described as "very tough."

Shortly before I took the stand they met with the judge and afterward seemed even gloomier, saying that the judge had insisted that a judicial finding of mental illness had been made, and, according to the Dubina case, a strong case would have to be presented to overcome the original finding of mental illness.

I suggested to the attorneys first of all to emphasize that the original commitment occurred under the automatic commitment which might now be unconstitutional in view of the recent U. S. Supreme Court decision in the Baxtrom case. Furthermore, the Dubina case was in 1946, prior to the Baxtrom decision.

The attorneys did go on record regarding the constitutionality of Turner's commitment, whereupon the judge said, "Why didn't you bring that up at the beginning of this hearing? This was not part of your pleadings."

But the pleadings were amended to include this new issue. It was my belief that this was not good, as it would put pressure on the judge to recognize that there had been no judicial finding of mental illness, only an automatic commitment, and also to set him on notice that the case might be appealed if he ruled unfavorably.

During my direct examination I made the statement a few times that in this case there had been no finding of mental illness, either by psychiatrists or by the courts. I knew this would induce the judge to question me more on this issue, which he did. He started off rather aggressively at the end of my very mild cross-examination by saying, "Doctor, you testified at his original trial that he was insane. The court found him insane. How can you keep saying that he was not found mentally ill?"

I replied that the original trial merely established the fact that the prosecution did not have enough evidence to prove beyond a reasonable doubt that Mr. Turner had the requisite state of mind to sustain the charge of first degree murder in killing his mother. I said, "I respectfully disagree with the court that there was a finding of mental illness, since that was not even the issue at the time of the trial. The only issue before the court was the condition of Mr. Turner at the time of the act in terms of criminal responsibility."

At this point the judge clearly backed off, shook his head and said some words to the effect that maybe I was right. I knew at this point that our chances had improved significantly. Ultimately the judge decided that Turner should be discharged. There was an emotional outburst on the part of an attractive blond girl in the court as she and Turner embraced. He then introduced her to me, saying that they had met at the hospital and were planning to be married.

James Turner, at the age of twenty-two, in one tragic act broke civilization's two greatest taboos—murder and incest. He murdered his mother, then tried to have intercourse with her dead body. This is an extremely rare crime in our civilization or in any other.

The wish to commit incest is universal in the lives of children, a natural part of psychosexual development. It stems from the attachment to the parent of the opposite sex which, at a more mature stage, is transferred to someone outside the family. Unless seduced by a parent, a child rarely acts out the wish, which is soon buried in the unconscious, and, it is to be hoped, all conflicts are resolved. The question to be answered, since most persons cope with their Oedipal urges without feeling compelled to kill a parent and then trying to have intercourse with him or her, is: What took place in the psychosexual development of James Turner that made him unable to cope with his incestuous and murderous wishes of his early childhood?

On the surface, his crime appears to be a clear case of Oedipal desire run rampant, but many signs show that his wishes were those of an earlier time of life, before Oedipal stage, which in the child starts at about the age of four. For one thing, as his mother lay dead, he sucked her breasts, regressing to the level of an infant. He wanted nourishment from her. We have to surmise that something went wrong with his early feeding, either that he did not get enough physical and emotional nourishment or that he was indulged too much. In his homosexual acts with his brother as a boy, he speaks of "milking" the penis, the image of an infant sucking.

He says of his mother, after he killed her, that she "didn't feel," that "she was only a woman." This shows he thought of her as an object without feelings, which is how a baby thinks of its mother; she is there only to please and succor him, not entitled to emotions of her own.

His excessive drinking, which began at about the age of twelve, shows his desperate need for this very early emotional and physical nourishment at his mother's breasts. It was as though he could never get enough beer; he always had a bottle (or a can) in his mouth.

We might wonder if James, the third and last child, born to parents who obviously did not get along, was a wanted child. If his mother did not truly care whether, as a baby, he lived or died, he too would have this feeling about himself all through life. His father described him as a "strange, moody boy who would go for weeks without talking to anyone." James told me that he couldn't remember anything happy about his childhood. He had no hobbies, no interests; he only wanted to drink and have what passed for sexual intercourse with girls. In his attempts to rape girls, he ejaculated before he even penetrated them, another sign that emotionally he was still a child rather than a man who could satisfy a woman sexually.

He had extreme difficulty as a child separating from his mother. He cried the first day he was taken to school by his brother and had to be sent home. He said he always cried the first day of school thereafter. James Turner was an exceptionally dependent child and remained that way even though he became physically a man.

It is rare that a murder so clearly shows the close connection between sex and murder that may exist in the mind of the emotionally disturbed person, as well as so direct a revenge on the original target of love and hate—the mother. James both desired his mother sexually as the object of his early love and hated her intensely because of his severe early frustrations. He hated her because she aroused unbearable anxiety in him.

We can think of James's unconscious as a whirlpool of murderous and sexual desires that overrode all his attempts to use reason. We all have such desires, but they become intolerable only when control of them is lacking because of great hatred or frustration carried from childhood. Love permits us the poise to control our hate. Lacking this love, it cost James a great price over the years to control his murderous feelings, ones he seemed unable to express even in small degree against those who inspired his hate.

There undoubtedly was great hate in the household, of which somehow James felt more the target than his brother or sister, perhaps because he was more unwanted. His parents may have been more compatible earlier in their marriage. Contrary to what James told Dr. Dukay, that his parents had gotten along well, he revealed in his letter to me that only a week before the killing his father had fought angrily with his mother and told her to pack and leave the house (she went upstairs to the bedroom but did not leave). Consistent with the father's tyrannical manner, he told her to leave, whereas most men would have walked out themselves rather than throw the woman out as though she were a slave. When his father told James he wanted a divorce, James said this was a "shock" to him. Here we see another important key to why he may have murdered his mother. He was now faced with losing the most important person in the world to him. One way not to lose her would be to kill her. A child has the fantasy that if he can destroy and devour his mother, taking her inside psychologically, she will remain his forever. Rather than let his mother walk out of the house and away from him, James, in the grip of an unconscious fantasy, may have thought that by killing her he would keep her with him.

His father appears to have been a cruel man, as many alcoholics are. James remembered his father slapping his sister as one of his few childhood memories. Undoubtedly his father, when drunk, hit his mother, as James did his wife. His father allowed him, at the age of sixteen, to be taken to a house of detention, wanting to punish him for setting the fire and stealing, rather than trying to help his troubled son in a constructive, thoughtful way by getting psychological help.

James's dreams while he was in jail tell of his inner feelings and wishes, ones he dared not face consciously. They show his terror of the people in his life—a Frankenstein, his father; a lion, his mother; people "with real ugly faces," all out to kill him. His dreams show both his fear of his parents and his own hidden desire for revenge, for in a dream the dreamer plays all the roles.

In one dream, his brother Tony was to execute a man on his knees (James had been on his knees when he kissed his mother's breasts, a taboo act for a grown man). His brother shot the man in the back of the head but did not kill him and had to shoot the man again, then ran away (as James had shot his mother twice, then ran away).

In another dream he was chased by a dragon, "fire and all," a monster breathing fire (his image of his father, or mother, or both). In a third, his father poured "a tub of bricks" on him, wanting to destroy him (perhaps the detention home was built of bricks). In a fourth dream, James was standing in a high building with his back toward the window when someone shot him in the stomach and he fell out the window. In another, a sheriff was trying to rape James's wife. All his dreams were of shootings, executions, rape—danger and violence.

He was exceptionally frank about his sexual activities, which started early. He did not want a close relationship with any girl but liked to be admired by many. He said, "I just could not stay with one girl." He said of school that the reason he liked it was that he could "go with girls." In the elementary grades he spoke of wanting to have intercourse with his teacher and a girl student whom he asked if she knew what "fuck" meant. He had intercourse regularly when he was fifteen. When he had his own apartment he stood naked in front of the window as the girls walked by on their way home from school, explaining, "I just wanted them to see me," obviously meaning his penis; otherwise he wouldn't have undressed.

His relationship with his wife was a selfish, sadistic one. He did not have sex with her for months because "I didn't want to give her the satisfaction of knowing I wanted her." He masturbated in the bathroom rather than give her pleasure. He cheated on her with other women. He struck his wife "quite a lot" before and after marriage because "she could hurt my feelings, and I don't like to be hurt" (which was also the way he felt about his mother).

His setting fire to a haystack when he burglarized a farm near his home tells us something of his destructive wishes, as does the fact that he said he and his wife would "naturally" leave their home, even during dinner, whenever they would hear a fire truck go past the door.

James was sexually precocious but in an infantile way. He got a married woman pregnant and did not care what happened to her or the baby. He tried to destroy his wife and unborn child. He both feared and hated women, as his actions show, the final proof being his destruction of the woman who had given him life. He says he molested his mother sexually because "it seemed the logical thing to do." If he was carrying out his father's wish to get rid of her, playing his father's role, it would be "logical" for him to have sex with his mother as his father had done, in that peculiar "logic" of the unconscious which knows no conscience, only desire.

As a boy, he indulged in what was probably excessive homosexual play with his older brother. His mother's reaction when she came upon her two sons masturbating is interesting— she said not a word but asked them to get dressed. James speaks of her "watching" them, as though she were a compliant witness to the act. His one later homosexual experience was unsatisfactory. He and his cousin, a boy his own age to whom he was very close, would only pretend to be homosexuals, but in such pretense one sees the wish. James was drawn to older men, perhaps substitutes for his older brother, with whom he had had sexual play in earlier years.

He had no sense of what other people thought of as right or wrong. When his wife became pregnant, he cheated on her with another girl, then tried to injure her so she would lose the baby, dragging her along the road when her hand got caught in the door of his car. His feelings of intense jealousy at the thought of a rival, his unborn child, probably stirred up feelings connected to his mother and hatred of his rivals at home, his brother and sister. It didn't occur to him that a prospective father does not kill his wife and unborn child. Or that a son does not kill his mother and try to have intercourse with her. All he was aware of was that he was in the grip of a depression and was going to kill either himself or his mother—thoughts of murder and suicide often accompany each other. He did not consciously know why he killed her, as he said. All he knew was the feeling of unbearable anxiety.

Why did he kill his mother at this particular time, if she had always made him anxious? A number of stress situations were now added to those that had disturbed him over the years: the pregnancy of his wife, her intention to divorce him, abandonment by his girl friend, loss of his job, and, what may have been the most important of all, his father's intention to throw his mother out of the house and divorce her. Now he not only would lose the most important person in his life but would be left to live alone in the house with his father. He may have feared he would kill his father, a punitive man who had sent him to the detention school "to teach him a lesson," a man who kept a shotgun in the basement to kill innocent deer, a man who drank a lot. James said of his father that "he had been drinking most of the day" before he told his wife to get out.

Though it seems a minor cause, the car breaking down depressed him, he said. In the unconscious, a car may be an extension of the self, and James may have felt a loss of power, crippled like his car, broken, unmanly. He couldn't even pay his bills, as his mother accusingly pointed out.

His mother's words, without her knowing it, may have triggered her own death. She said to her son reprovingly, when he told her he had quit his job, "That's no way to pay your bills," expressing anger at his irresponsibility about financial matters. It was as though she were saying to him, "You're not a man." A man earns money to support a woman, a man has a penis, and in James's unconscious it may have been as if his mother were taking away his manhood, and he felt castrated. He had always felt castrated, as shown by his sexual behavior and his rage at and fear of women. He killed his mother out of rage for saying he was not a man, rage at depriving him too early in life of her breast. He never was able to acquire the emotional strength to cope with the fantasies all children have but which come under the control of the ego as the child learns about reality.

Too, he may have unconsciously been carrying out his father's wish to get rid of his mother, identifying with the aggressor, the "boss" of the house, his ideal of "man." To him, and to his father, a woman had no right to feelings, perhaps even to be alive if she was too frustrating; she was an inferior, castrated creature.

He says, "I don't know why I killed her, just that I couldn't think very good that day. . . . I felt like I was half asleep." When we are half asleep our unconscious takes over and our inhibitions become lowered, as when we drink excessively. He said, "I always drank quite a lot before I could do anything. I guess for courage. Also, I didn't really care about anything when I was drunk."

He said he intended to commit suicide and knew he had to "do something bad" to justify the contemplated suicide, but actually the wish "to do something bad" came first and then the need to punish himself by suicide.

He could channel neither his sexual nor his aggressive drive. One wonders if he could have been sexually overstimulated by his mother when a boy, whether she, like some mothers, was very lax in asking her sons to control their sexual activities, perhaps fearing to do so (as when she "watched" them masturbate). Perhaps she even walked around the house exposing her body seductively, without being aware of how she aroused feelings of desire in her youngest son. James says he looked up his mother's dress when he was a boy, as most boys either do or wish to do out of natural sexual curiosity, but her reaction may have been one that further excited his fantasies rather than helped him control his feelings.

This is not to condone but to understand the many complicated roots of murder. Something haunted this family, over and above most families, that made James feel unmanly and unworthy, that perpetuated emotional infancy in him, that thwarted his normal psychosexual development, making it impossible for him to assume the responsibility of young manhood.

While early traumatic events are important, it is also day-to-day living with the kind of disturbed parents who cause the trauma that creates emotional illness. The parent who will strike a child unnecessarily, or seduce him in subtle ways, is the parent who, in day-to-day living, will provide an aura of cruelty and unbearable frustration rather than love and tenderness. And from such an aura springs the hate that triggers murder.

4

"Until Death Do Us Part"

Angus Walsh left the automotive factory where he worked in Flint, Michigan, to stop at the bank, as he usually did on Fridays, to deposit his weekly check. It was late in the afternoon of August 20, 1971.

He stood in the bank and endorsed the check. He made out the deposit slip. Then he noticed that recently there had been two large withdrawals entered in the bank book. One was for $500, the other for $1500. The account was a joint one with his wife Ellen. He wondered why she had taken out two such large sums.

He called her at once from a phone at the bank. He asked, "Ellen, what did you do with the money you withdrew from our account?"

"I'll explain when you get home," she said. Then she added, "There's a man waiting for you here."

"Who is it?" he asked.

"I think he wants to talk about going hunting with you," she said.

"It must be Jim." He had spoken to Jim a few days before about a bear-hunting trip; the season was approaching.

As he drove home, he thought Ellen probably had given the

116

$500 to her brother, who was building a new house and had mentioned that he needed that amount to finish it, and the $1500 to her brother-in-law, who had told her he needed a loan for that amount to put down on a new home.

Angus parked the car in his driveway and stepped out of it. A man walked across the lawn toward him. The man was not Jim.

The man handed him a large envelope. Then he shook Angus's hand and said, "Don't do anything drastic."

Puzzled, Angus opened the envelope. He took out a sheaf of papers. At the top he saw in large letters the word "divorce," then his name, then Ellen's name. At the sight of the word "divorce," he felt his stomach churn, as though he were going to throw up. A surge of panic hit him, as if everything in the world were being taken from him.

He folded the papers and walked into the house. In the living room he saw his three children, Deborah, eleven, Mary, ten, and David, five, and his wife, just sitting. The three children looked at him in repressed alarm. Ellen's face was stoical, unmoving.

He noticed his suitcase, also sitting in the living room, a strange sight. He turned to Ellen and said, "Why are you doing this? Please don't do it."

She just shook her head hopelessly, as if it were too much effort to speak to him.

"Please," he begged. "You can't do this to me."

At that moment her mother walked into the house, the person to whom Ellen always rushed with the children whenever she and he had had a fight. Ellen said to the children, "Go outside and play," and they stood up and ran out of the room as if they could not wait to reach the safety of the outdoors.

Angus turned to his mother-in-law and asked, still not understanding, "Why is Ellen doing this?"

Her mother answered, "She says she doesn't love you."

He turned to Ellen. "Why? Why don't you love me?"

Ellen refused to answer.

He said to her mother, "Well, if she's going to leave me, please take her out of here. Take her to your home. Just take her away." He felt he could not handle what was happening, that if Ellen stayed near him he might do something terrible.

He was not going to leave. If Ellen wanted a divorce, she

would be the one to go. He lifted his suitcase—it was heavy, as she had packed it fully—and took it back upstairs. He placed it on his bed and returned downstairs.

Deborah ran into the house breathlessly, saying in excitement, "Mary and Davy are climbing the tree after Tiny. They might fall." Tiny was their new kitten.

He followed Deborah outside, still numb, moving like an automaton. The shock of Ellen's betrayal had taken all feeling away. Mary and David, trying to rescue the kitten, were climbing a large maple. He told them, "Come down before you get hurt. Tiny will come down when she's ready."

As he walked back to the house he thought, This is my house, I built it for my family, Ellen is my wife, and I am not going to let her leave me. Ever. We have too much at stake.

He said to Ellen in front of her mother, "I'm not leaving. And I don't want you to leave."

Her mother stood up. "I'm going home," she said. "You two argue it out."

He walked his mother-in-law to the car. He asked her, "Mom, do you believe Ellen's going to go through with it?"

"Yes, I think she is," said his mother-in-law.

"Then please take her home with you," he begged again.

She shook her head, as though the whole affair were no business of hers.

He said, with a sigh, "Then I'd better get my suitcase and go." He was afraid of what he might do if he remained. Ellen and her mother did not seem to realize how upset he was.

Her mother stepped into the car and drove off, and he walked back to the house. Inside, he again pleaded with Ellen, like a small child who refuses to take "no" from his mother when he wants something desperately, something he feels he cannot live without.

"Ellen, don't do it, don't do it," he kept saying.

Her face was set, her mouth unyielding, her blue eyes cold. She said not a word, as though she were beyond argument.

He walked upstairs to his room. He opened the packed suitcase lying on his bed. On the very top Ellen had placed his license for deer hunting; he had planned to leave September 28 for a week's vacation. But she had forgotten one important item for the hunting trip. He walked across the room to the bureau to get his lip ice, for use if the cold wind in the woods chapped his lips.

He opened the bureau drawer, saw the lip ice, picked it up and put it in his pocket. Then he saw, also lying in the drawer, his gun. He picked up the gun, put it in the suitcase, shut the suitcase.

He walked downstairs slowly, carrying the heavy suitcase into the kitchen, where Ellen was seated at the table. He put the suitcase on the kitchen counter. Deborah was there. He asked if she had fed the dog, and she said, "No, but I will," and went outside to the yard.

Ellen had not fixed supper, as she usually did at this hour. It was as though she were refusing to feed the children or herself until he left—as though she wanted him to starve.

He noticed that the divorce papers were now on top of the refrigerator; he must have put them there when he left the house to get Mary and David out of the tree. He asked Ellen, "Do you still want me to take those papers?" and pointed to them.

"Yes," she said.

He reached up, took the divorce papers off the refrigerator, opened his suitcase and started to put them inside.

As he did so, he saw his gun.

He picked it up and walked toward Ellen. He stood close to her, about two feet away, and pointed the gun at her, almost as though he were showing it to her defiantly. He said once again, "Ellen, won't you change your mind?"

She seemed to do two things at once. She screamed "Deborah!" as though for help. And she pushed at the gun, as if to get it out of the way, as if it were a toy gun, not real but repulsive to her anyhow.

At that moment, he felt the gun go off, almost automatically. He was not even aware of pressing the trigger. A bullet hit her in the middle of the forehead. He thought it was almost as if this had to happen, he had to do it, there was no other way, and he had known it from the moment the stranger handed him the divorce papers.

The next thing he knew, his younger daughter Mary stood in front of him screaming hysterically. Then he saw her run out of the kitchen door. She joined the other two children in the yard, and they all started to run away from the house in the direction of the Smiths, who lived across the street in a trailer. The children spent a lot of time with Ruth Smith, who seemed to love them. She was a registered nurse and sometimes watched them when Ellen went shopping.

A busy highway, with trucks speeding along it, separated the two houses. He was afraid the children might get hurt, so, gun in hand, he ran after them. He could not catch them but noted they had made it safely to the other side and were running into the trailer.

He crossed the highway, and on the lawn in front of the trailer he saw Arthur Smith, who had walked out of the trailer to meet him. He handed Arthur the gun and said, "I believe I just shot my wife."

Then he entered the trailer. He saw his children cowering in a corner, Ruth trying to comfort them. He told the children gently, "I had to do it. I hope you can forgive me."

Ruth asked, "Can I go to your house? Maybe I can help Ellen."

"She's dead," he said. "You can't help her."

"I'm going to call the police," Ruth said.

He watched her dial a number. Then he took the phone from her. He wanted to turn himself in.

A voice on the phone, a state trooper, asked him, "What happened?"

He said, "My name is Angus Walsh. I live at . . ." and he gave the address. Then he said, "I'm sane now. I've shot my wife. Six times." He wondered why he said six times; he only remembered firing the gun once, and then it did not seem as if he had fired it but that he was being told he had to do it.

He added, "Don't come with a bunch of sirens. I know I killed her." The police did not have to storm the house and take him; he was perfectly willing to surrender.

When he hung up, Ruth said, "I want to walk back to the house with you," like a registered nurse doing her duty at the scene of an accident.

They left the children in the trailer. As they reached his house he turned to Ruth and said, "I don't want you to go in. You can't do anything for her."

He remembered that nobody had set out water for the dog. He walked to the back yard, picked up the empty pan, and took it into the kitchen. Ellen was still sitting at the table, lifeless, the bullet hole in her forehead, blood streaming down her face, over her dress, onto the floor.

He walked over to Ellen. He said to her, "Why did you do it?"

Then he filled the dog's pan with water and took it back to the yard.

After the state trooper arrived and read him his rights as they stood outside the house, they entered the kitchen. Angus wanted a drink of water; his mouth felt as if it were stuffed with cotton. But he did not get himself a drink.

Instead, he walked over to his wife, kissed her on the neck, and said, "Ellen, it doesn't matter, but I still love you."

◇◇◇◇◇◇◇

Frederick E. Salim, the attorney who was to defend Angus Walsh, asked me to examine Angus and make a psychiatric evaluation as to his sanity at the time of the murder. Angus was brought to my office under guard, and I tape-recorded an interview that lasted two sessions.

Angus was a tall, thin man, with a face that looked as though he once might have been a farmer—a gaunt face that seemed haunted even at the age of thirty-two. He had brown eyes that seemed shy but looked directly at me most of the time he answered my questions.

He asked me, "Where do you want to start?"

"Start anywhere you think is important—wherever you think the whole thing started, whatever led up to it in your mind," I said.

He paused for a moment, then said, "The man handed me the divorce papers, and from there on I was irrational. I went into a shock, you might say. An emotional state. We'd been married twelve years—what else can I say? All I could see was the big word—divorce—divorce—divorce."

He described how he had "begged and begged" his wife not to go through with the divorce, saying, "Don't do this to me.

Ellen, why are you doing this to me? Why? Why don't you love me?"

Then he told how he had pleaded with his mother-in-law to take Ellen away with her, adding, "They didn't seem to know how upset I was. I guess I knew in my own mind."

He said he thought of killing himself but told himself, "I'm not going to commit suicide."

"When was that?" I asked.

"I thought there was one bullet left, and I put the gun to my head and pulled the trigger, but the gun didn't go off. That's why I knew I shot her six times. I always kept the gun fully loaded." And he started to cry uncontrollably.

After he recovered, he said, "I love my wife. I want her alive today. Why did she try to destroy me this way? Why did she try to destroy me and my family—everything I built up for twelve years?"

"Why do you suppose she did?" I asked.

"I don't know. I honestly don't know." His voice was puzzled.

"Tell me about your marriage," I said.

"I've been married twelve years," he said, then stopped. He added reluctantly, "It wasn't too great from the start, I guess. Even on our honeymoon."

"What happened on the honeymoon?" I asked.

"Sex-wise, I guess maybe I was too—I don't know. I remember her saying, 'All you want to do is roll me over and do it.' And I said, 'My God, it's a honeymoon, what do you want to do?' She was a little upset that I wasn't quite so romantic, I guess, as she thought I should be."

"Romantic means what, to you?" I asked.

"I don't know. I thought I was romantic. Maybe she wanted me to be a little more romantic. I loved her and thought that's all there was to it."

"How did you meet her?" I asked.

"Through her sister. I went with her sister Kate first, on a couple of dates. Kate was three years younger than I was. Then she introduced me to Ellen, who was only three months younger than me. I started dating her. All through that year of high school, my last, and her next to last, we went together. We were married when she graduated in 1959."

He was silent again, then returned to thoughts of their honeymoon, saying, "There was some difficulty about sex at first, on our honeymoon. But then, as married life goes, we got along pretty good for about a year and a half. Though even then our sex life wasn't too great, I guess."

"When you say 'not too great,' would you tell me a little more specifically what you mean?" I asked.

"Our sexual relationship was rather cold. It seemed to be like a job. Yes, in a sense, like a job."

"For whom was it a job?"

"For both of us, at first, I believe. I thought, Well, this will gradually work itself out. By then we had one child."

"How often would sex take place?"

"If I was lucky, I figured I got it about once a week for a while. Then it got less, maybe once every two weeks, which I always thought wasn't right. But I learned to live with it."

"Meaning you didn't like it?"

"I didn't like it but I loved the woman, regardless of what sex with her was like. I figured eventually it was going to work out. In the first year we had Deborah. My wife had her by Caesarean section. In fact, all three of the children were Caesarean sections. When Ellen was pregnant with David, the doctor recommended she have an operation to tie her tubes. He said the delivery of the baby and the tying of the tubes could be all one operation, and the tubes could be rejoined later if she wanted more children."

"Usually more than three Caesarean sections are not advisable," I said.

"The babies came so close together, I guess," he said. "Even the doctor who recommended the operation was of a faith that doesn't believe in it. He gave us the name of another doctor to do the operation."

"You mean the first doctor was Catholic?"

"Right."

"You are not?"

"No. Neither was my wife. The Catholic doctor recommended the operation, he said, because Ellen had had rheumatic fever and had a slight heart murmur. The operation was performed, and at the same time, fortunately, we had a boy."

"Did you and your wife ever fight in the early years?" I asked.

"Just after our first baby was born. On Valentine's Day, when I thought things were going along fine, Ellen filed for divorce. She had been working, and I thought this was making life rough for her. She worked days and I worked nights at the time. We were living in a trailer. She went home to her mother with the baby. I didn't know what to do, so I went to the home of one of my brothers. I saw a lawyer and told him I did not want a divorce, and I wanted my little daughter back. Though I didn't know it, Ellen was pregnant again. I went to her mother's house, and Ellen wasn't home. I told my mother-in-law I was taking Deborah back with me. The next night I had papers served on me. The court said I had to return my daughter. So I took her back and pleaded with Ellen, begged her to come home, but she wouldn't.

"So for a while I moved into my mother's house. My dad had passed away—he had told me not to marry Ellen. I kept calling Ellen, pleading with her to come back, and visited her at her mother's house. Finally we were reconciled. I told her I wanted her to quit working. She stayed on the job until her pregnancy leave, and that was the last she ever worked.

"Things went along pretty good then, I thought; the children were getting older, we had a lot of fun with our two daughters. I believed I was happy; at least, I thought I was. Our sex life wasn't the greatest, but I had no remorse. The relationship was still a little on the cold side, but like I say, I learned to love my wife the way she was. Then, all of a sudden, there was no sex life at all. Maybe once a month, then maybe once every two months."

"You mean she would not want sex?"

"Right. And then, whenever she did give in, it was very regimental—almost like a routine, as though she never really enjoyed it. But I kept telling her, 'I love you, I'm going to live with you.' And so we went on. I bought thirty-three acres with dozens of apple trees on it, and we moved the trailer out. I chopped the trees down myself, worked the land the best I could with a little tractor I bought. It was my dream to have a home and children. We had the house built the following spring. The contractor, my wife and I went over the plans several times to make sure they were what Ellen and I wanted. Things were going along pretty good. Like I say, our sex life could have been a lot better, but it was no grounds for a divorce, not from my estimation.

"Then all of a sudden, this last six months, Ellen started saying, 'I don't love you, I don't love you.' I just couldn't make myself believe it. And then I got hit with the divorce papers."

"Do you suppose your wife was saying 'I don't love you' because she didn't?" I asked.

"This is true, possibly. But I just couldn't make myself believe it. Even though I think there were two or three incidents where she might have been cheating on me."

"What kind of incidents are you talking about?" I asked.

"She went up north with a 'girl friend' whom I had never heard her mention and stayed away a couple of days, supposedly to clean the girl friend's cabin. Then, another time, she had keys to a strange car. I asked her what she was doing with that car. She said she was taking it to the husband of a friend of hers. Little things like that happened."

"Why didn't you ask her about them?" I said.

"I did. When she told me she was taking the car to the husband as a favor for her friend, I thought, Okay, she's doing this for a friend."

"What's changed your mind about the incidents now?" I said. "You seem to have second thoughts."

"Now I have reason to believe maybe she was going out with other men. Earlier, I didn't."

"How do you know she was going out with other men?" I asked.

"I don't know."

"When she said she went up north for a few days with a 'girl friend' you didn't know, didn't you look into this?"

"No, sir, I did not."

"You had no suspicions?"

"I had no suspicions. I figured she was going up north for the weekend to help her girl friend clean the cabin. Maybe there was another man, maybe several other men. And this is why she kept saying she didn't love me.''

"When did the trip to the cabin take place?''

"The early part of this summer. June.''

The reason Angus now had for believing his wife had been unfaithful was that after her death an album turned up among her possessions which contained photographs of herself posing with different men and of the places they had visited together—a self-incriminating document of her infidelities. Angus probably sensed, when his wife asked for a divorce, that she was in love with someone else, maybe the man she had obviously slept with at the cabin "up north.''

Angus referred to the bank book, saying, "She was being awful funny about it. I was a great one for putting money away. She would say, 'Why do you always want a security blanket?' I said, 'I'm trying to put something aside to buy a new car.' I rebuilt the engine on our old car, even repaired the truck when it went bad.''

It turned out that his wife had withdrawn the $2,000 in preparation for her divorce, advised to do so by her attorney.

In talking about the day he was handed the divorce papers, Angus mentioned the man who had served him, warning, "Don't do anything drastic.''

I asked, "Why would he say that?''

"I don't know why a man would say that. I opened the papers to read them, and when I saw what they were, he was gone.''

"Maybe he had some experience with similar cases where the husband lost his temper,'' I suggested.

"This could be. Maybe he knew me better than I knew myself. Why? Why did I have to do it? That's what I want to know. I can't understand it.''

"What thoughts do you have?''

"It just seemed like I was caught in a vise. Or in a balloon with something, or somebody, pushing in on it. Everything let loose all at once. I don't understand it myself. I wish I knew.''

"Couldn't you imagine yourself divorced from your wife?''

"No. No!''

"Why not?''

"I don't want a divorce.''

It was as though he were still denying his wife was dead, that he had killed her.

"Why not?" I asked. "It wasn't such a happy marriage."

"It was my home. My children. And my wife. And I loved her. And that's all there is to it. I didn't want a divorce. No divorce." Quietly adamant.

"Why did you love her?"

"She was beautiful—to me. She was everything I had. Regardless of sex, I still loved the woman. I don't know why. Why do you love something? Why do you love a dog? You don't love a dog for sex."

"If the dog bit you, you might not love it."

"If a dog bites you, you cuff him up a little bit. Maybe you correct him. Maybe in a sense I thought I was correcting her."

Then he added in sorrow, "But what a way to correct it!"

"Why couldn't you picture yourself divorced from her?" I asked.

"I don't know. I guess I just didn't believe in divorce."

"She wanted a divorce. You might not want it, but she wanted it. Your marriage was not a happy one. Why couldn't you take a divorce?"

"I don't know. I can't tell you why. I can't understand why myself. If she were alive today, I would fight the divorce with everything I have. Because I love her."

I asked, wanting to know more about his background, "Where were you born?"

"I was born right in a home in this town."

"Tell me a little bit about your parents."

"My mother was a housewife. Mom was always a hearty individual. She liked to do things, like go camping. My two brothers and I peddled papers to make money. My dad worked in the shop at Buick, at first nights, the third shift, then days."

"What kind of man was your father?" I asked.

"He was the best guy I ever knew. He took me hunting with him. He was like my companion. He steered me everyplace I went. I wish he were alive today. In fact, I miss him more than anybody else, I guess, other than my wife."

"Did he die suddenly?"

"He was always in good health until the week he went into the hospital. He had cancer. He was in about six weeks. They operated, but there was cancer all through his lungs and esophagus, and he died."

"Was he a strict father?"

"No, the man was not strict. He taught me how to save money and make things. He taught me how to make arrows, train a dog, and he got me a job."

"What would happen if you got out of line?"

"I don't believe my dad ever laid a hand on me other than a pat on my butt when I needed it when I was a little guy, maybe when I was spitting spinach out on the back porch. I believe all Dad expected was an up-and-coming son. I worked from the time I was nine years old, which doesn't give a guy too much time for childhood. I collected money for my one brother every Thursday and Friday night, and Saturday I'd pick up the stragglers for him. This was on a route of about 120 to 146 customers. When I was twelve I took over the route and handled it until I was eighteen. Dad was trying to get me into Buick as a pattern maker, and I also enrolled for college. I went to college that fall. Then, in January, the apprenticeship came through, and I was hired in Buick and have been there ever since."

"Have you ever been in trouble with the law?"

"No. I've never been drunk. I have got speeding tickets. I had one accident where a man turned left in front of me. My license was suspended for thirty days. Nothing since but some speeding tickets, but not more than an average of about five in twelve years."

"Have you been in the military?"

"No. Never was. I went down to the draft board and signed up but never was called."

"Are you the kind of man who gets into fights easily?"

"I only recall one fight in my life, when I was a kid in the seventh grade in high school. Another kid threw a chalk eraser across the room at me. It bounced and hit me either on the head or on the shoulders. We got out in the hall and scuffled, and I ended up with a bloody nose. And a whack on the tailbone from the principal of the school. I can remember the whack on the rear end better than the bloody nose."

"Have you ever beaten your wife?"

"I struck her the first time she wanted a divorce, when we were arguing just before Mary was born. I shoved my fist through the little glass window on the door. I smacked that rather than hit her. But I also grabbed her. She said I choked her, but that's a matter of opinion. I don't believe I ever choked anybody."

"That's the only time?"

"There was one other time I did strike my wife, back possibly two years ago, or a year ago. I believe it was in the warmer weather. We had an argument. She wanted to leave me again. I think she was going up the steps to get her clothes, and I said, 'Why do you have to take my kids from me?' Every time she left, she took my kids from me. She tried to kick me in the groin, but her foot hit the inside of my leg. I reached out and slapped her. And she went home to mama."

"Did she go back to her mother frequently?"

"In our twelve years of marriage, I believe she went home possibly four times."

"She felt you were in the wrong in striking her?"

"I know myself I was wrong in striking her even though she kicked me. But why should a man hit a woman? Men don't do that, that's all."

"You feel a man can be attacked by a woman and he shouldn't do anything?"

"I believe a man should be able to protect himself from a woman without harming her. I never have, other than the one time I did slap her for kicking me."

"So she went to her mother. How did she get back?"

"I went and got her. Every time she's left, I've always gone and got her. One time I hitchhiked. I called her up and told her when I finished with the chores—I had to get the soybeans in from the field—and got the dog fed, I would hitchhike to her mother's home so I could ride back with her. It was late at night by the time I finished. I walked most of the way, twenty-six miles, and got there about one or two in the morning."

"Why couldn't she drive home?"

"I wanted to drive home with her. So I told her I'd come and get her. I've always gone and got her."

"You would walk twenty-six miles to get her when she had the car?"

"It's a verified fact. Her mother will tell you this. Why I did it, I don't know."

"You are a glutton for punishment, isn't that true?" I said.

"Maybe this is the way you see it, but to me I wasn't."

"What would you call it?"

"I thought I was showing her a sign of affection. I thought maybe she'd learn I did love her. Why take another car, or why take a motorcycle or something, when I could drive back with her?"

"You had a car?"

"I had another car sitting right in the driveway. I also had two motorcycles."

"Why didn't you take one of them?"

"I didn't want to. I wanted to be with my wife coming home. Can you understand that?"

"No, I can't," I said, realizing he was undoubtedly punishing himself for his guilt at striking her, wanting to appear so submissive that she would not regret coming home to him again.

"That's all I can tell you. That I wanted to be with my wife coming home."

I asked, "Where were the children?"

"They were with her. When I walked into her mother's home, Ellen was sleeping on the floor in the front room. We lay there on the floor and more or less made up. No love, no sex involved—why push things when you know it isn't best? But we had sex the next morning when I took off from work. I loved her no matter what she did."

"Your wife is dead and you tell me that you loved her, but I have the impression that she wasn't very nice to you," I said. "Would you agree?"

"I'd have to agree with you now, yes. But then, no. If she were sitting right here and I was talking to her, I'd love her, and that's all there is to it. I don't know why, but like I say, I love her." Then he added in a childlike way, "If there were only some way possible I could put the breath of life into the woman. My wife. My woman. Ellen."

I asked, "How come you had a gun?"

"I always had guns. I've got several guns."

"What do you need a gun for?"

"Hunting."

"A pistol?"

"I use it for running trap lines. I know it's a big one, but it's what I always wanted. I always wanted a .357. I own a .22 also."

"Why did you keep it loaded in the drawer?"

"There was a break-in in the house, and thieves stole a pistol exactly like the one I have."

"So you put another one, loaded, back into the drawer, ready for them to come again?"

"More or less. I kept it loaded there in the drawer in case somebody got messing around the house. I don't think I'd ever shoot anybody with it. All I wanted it for was more or less protection."

"The previous gun didn't give you much protection. Thieves broke in and stole it."

"I wasn't home."

"You might not have been home the second time."

"That's true."

"What did you need the gun for?" I persisted.

"Like I say, the only thing I had it for was hunting."

"Did you use that particular gun for hunting?"

"I took it out west on one of three or four trips."

"Was it a registered gun?"

"Yes. I had fourteen guns. I was more or less a collector."

"I think you should be afraid of guns," I said.

"Why should I be afraid of a gun?" he asked.

"If it hadn't been for your gun, you would not be sitting here now talking to me, would you?"

"I don't think it was the gun." He sounded thoughtful.

"If you didn't have a gun, you would have maybe slapped your wife but you would not have killed her, would you?"

"I didn't want to do her personal harm."

"If you did not have the gun, you would not have gone and gotten a gun, would you?"

"Maybe I would have gone and gotten something else. I don't know," he said.

"Like what?"

"I don't know. I've always owned a gun. You're suggesting that if I didn't have a gun, I might have slapped her like I did once before. But I didn't want to hurt her. Can you understand that?"

"I do understand. But what I don't understand is that you are still not aware of the fact that the gun had a great deal to do with affecting what you did to your wife."

"I've handled many guns. I've shot trap. I've shot pheasants. I've shot deer. And I know the potential of the rifle and pistol. I even load bullets.''

"You're talking about the technique of using a gun," I pointed out. "I'm talking about the fact that if the gun had not been there, most likely you would not be here now.''

"Probably not," he said. "Probably if the gun hadn't been there, I think I'd have walked out. Because I was on the way out. I was coming downstairs with the suitcase.''

"That's what I am saying," I said. Then I asked, "When you reached for the gun, what did you have in mind?''

"I wanted to frighten her. I picked the gun up and said to her, 'Please don't do it, Ellen.' If she saw the gun, I thought, maybe she would understand how much she was pushing me. I wanted to get to her. When I picked the gun up, I wanted my wife to see how emotionally she had me pushed. I reached into the suitcase and picked the gun up because I wanted her to see how desperate I was, that I didn't want a divorce. I kept saying to her, 'I don't want it, I don't want it, Ellen. Please don't do it.' And knowing she was going to do it, no matter what I said, something snapped.''

"When she pushed you away, you mean?''

"Pushed my hand away. Roughly. With both her hands. Hard as she could.''

"What was she trying to tell you?''

"It was like she didn't believe me. And if she didn't believe me, she didn't want me. It was like she was saying, 'Get out of here. Go away.' And at that, the gun swung back and it went off, just like it was almost automatic. I don't shoot a pistol that way, you understand; you've got to swing a pistol back. I can tell you where the first bullet hit, but I don't know about the others. The next thing that happened, I saw my daughter screaming.''

He had no memory of the other five bullets he had fired into his wife's face, two hitting her in the left temple, two in the left cheek just below the eye, one in the corner of her right eye. Two of the bullets exited into her right shoulder.

In my evaluation of Mr. Walsh's sanity at the time of the murder, I wrote Mr. Salim that I found Walsh cooperative and that he showed "no gross psychopathology," that he understood the charges placed against him and could cooperate with his counsel; there was no evidence of any psychotic illness and no doubt whatsoever of his ability to stand trial.

I also wrote: "In the interview situation he became, on a number of occasions, quite emotional, cried, and gave expression to profound remorse, depression, and suicidal ideas. He gave a history of having been the product of a rather uneventful childhood. He was raised in a strict environment, believing in hard work, and never causing his parents or school authorities any kind of difficulty. He married Ellen, his high school sweetheart, and has been a devoted, dependent, submissive husband for the subsequent twelve years. The relationship to Ellen is clearly and unmistakably a sadomasochistic one, as illustrated, for example, by the following episode which occurred a number of years ago:

"There is some minor disagreement. Ellen tries to kick him in the groin. He slaps her (the only time in his life). She goes with the children to her mother's, twenty-six miles away. He calls his wife, apologizes, and states he will hitchhike to pick her up as soon as he does the chores at home. He does so, walking a major portion of the distance and arriving in the early hours of the morning. All this is done in spite of the fact that he has another car and two motorcycles at home. He explains it by his desire to drive together with his wife and children. Quite obviously, it also is designed to satisfy his need to be punished.

"Throughout the marriage he has been subjected to abuse and sexual deprivation. Nevertheless, he professes an inexhaustible and unquestionable love for his wife. In 1961, when she requested a divorce, he begged her to reconsider, and through this approach and with considerable humiliation he was able to persuade her to return to him. Divorce has been a totally unacceptable, terrifying idea to him.

"The interview and the material indicate that he has been a rigid, highly conscientious individual. There is no record of any antisocial activities or proclivities. The interview, as well as the history, clearly establishes that he has a well-developed and rather strict conscience (superego) and certainly has no criminal propensities. There is no history of violence whatsoever. The only fight in his life occurred in high school. The episode of shooting occurred under traumatic and emotional circumstances which, in my judgment, provide a clear-cut basis for the defense of insanity under the irresistible-impulse concept. There is certainly no indication whatsoever, either from the history or from the report of witnesses or the investigating police officer, to indicate conscious preparation for the act. Therefore, it is, first of all, my professional opinion that there is no element of intent necessary for the charge of first degree murder. I am sure you are aware of the fact that psychiatric testimony is relevant to the issue of intent without the defense of insanity, and I have testified in such cases and have the appropriate legal citations. Obviously, the decision on this issue has to be left up to your judgment. Nevertheless, this particular part of my opinion might be useful in reducing the charge and obtaining bail for Mr. Walsh.

"I might add, in this context, that I do not consider him a dangerous person outside of a unique and highly emotional relationship like the one in relation to his wife."

✧✧✧✧✧✧✧

At the preliminary examination, held in court on September 7, 1971, Ruth Smith was called to the stand. She testified that she and her husband and the Walsh family were "good, friendly neighbors." She described the evening of August 20, 1971, when, at six o'clock, she heard "some banging noises" outside her trailer but thought it was her husband at work building their house behind the temporary mobile home.

Then her husband came to the door of the trailer and told her he had heard what sounded like shots. She saw the three Walsh children running up her driveway. She recalled, "They were crying and screaming that their daddy had a gun and he was shooting Mama."

She took the children inside the trailer and tried to comfort them. Deborah wanted to call her grandmother, but Ruth told her not to go near the phone, saying, "You're not going to call anybody right now." She told the court she did not know whether to believe what the children had said.

Then she looked up and saw Angus coming out the front door of his house and starting to walk toward her trailer, across the highway. When he reached her mailbox, she saw he had a gun in his hand. She said to her husband, "You go talk to Angus, and I'll keep the children in here."

Her husband went to speak to Angus, who handed him the gun. She left the children in the trailer and joined the two men. She heard Angus telling her husband, "It's all over. Ellen's dead. I know it."

She asked Angus if she could go and see if there was anything she could do for Ellen, since she was a registered nurse. But he told her not to go to the house, saying, "There's nothing you can do." She and her husband took him into the trailer. She said, "He told the children he had to do what he did. And he said, 'I hope you can forgive me.' "

She described how she dialed the police, whereupon Angus said, "I'll tell them everything, Ruth," and took the phone out of her hand. She said, "He told whoever answered the phone his name and address. He told them what had just happened. That he had shot his wife. And he said, 'I'm over at my neighbors' now, and I have my three children over here too.' And he said, 'I'm not going to do anything else. I'm not going to shoot myself.' He said, 'I'll be here waiting for you.' And he said, 'Don't come with any of your sirens screaming or anything else, either.' He said, 'She is dead, and I definitely know it.' "

She and Angus walked over to his house. She walked inside the garage and looked through a window into the kitchen, where she could see Ellen's body, "and I could see that she'd been shot, and I was quite sure she was dead, so I didn't go in."

She told Angus, "Angus, you're right," meaning Ellen was dead. He had the empty water pan for the dog in his hand; he said he was going to feed the dog, "and then he said he wanted to apologize to her. And he did go up on the back steps of their patio and he looked in at her, and he said, 'I'm sorry, honey.' He said, 'I loved you, but I had to do it.' "

She said she noticed an opened suitcase on the kitchen counter and asked, "Angus, whose suitcase is that?" and he told her it was his, "that she had it all packed for him and was kicking him out." Ruth said there were some papers lying by the suitcase and Angus "told me that those were the divorce papers he'd been served that night when he got home from work."

The state trooper soon arrived, and she did not stay at the house. Angus had asked her to call his brother to come and pick up the children, and she did this.

Under questioning by Mr. Salim, Ruth said she remembered telling the state trooper that she saw Ellen "sitting in the chair with her head slumped over her arm, and there was quite a bit of blood around." She also remembered that Angus had said to her about the shooting, "You don't miss at that close of a range with a gun like that."

She described Angus as appearing unexcited, normal, the way he always seemed, as though in control of himself. She recalled his saying to the state trooper on the phone, "I'm sane now."

Mr. Salim asked, "Did you personally observe an incident when Mr. Walsh was carried on the hood of a pickup truck from their home a distance down the road?"

"Yes," she said.

In response to Mr. Salim's asking her to tell about this incident, she described how one day the summer before, the three children ran over to her house when their parents were fighting. Ellen then backed the pickup truck into the Smiths' driveway, got out, and screamed for the children to get inside the truck, saying, "Come on, hurry up, or your daddy won't let me take you."

The three children ran out of the trailer and into the truck, and Ellen started out of the Smiths' driveway. Angus ran over and stood in front of the truck so Ellen could not drive any farther. She backed the truck up and started across the lawn. But he ran and stood in front of the truck. She backed it up again and started down the driveway. Then he climbed on the hood of the truck. She drove away with him on top of the hood. Ruth said, "She was going quite fast when she went out my driveway, and she just turned right on to M-13 and went down the road south."

Ruth was also asked if she had ever observed Ellen punishing the children. She said that she had but that the punishment had not been "unusual or harsh."

Then Mr. Salim said to her, "The next question has to do with whether or not you knew firsthand if Mrs. Walsh had a man friend, or men friends? From observation, or from your ability to hear or see, did you know whether or not Mrs. Walsh was associating with another man or men other than Mr. Walsh?"

"Yes, just on what I saw," she replied.

"What did you see?"

"I've seen a car over at their house with a man who got out and went into the house."

"More than one time?"

"Yes."

"Did you know the identity of the person?"

"I've never met the person."

"Do you know his name, though?"

"Only by what the children have told me."

"And would this have been at a time when Mr. Walsh, to your knowledge, was at work?"

"Yes."

"Had you ever said anything to Mr. Walsh?"

"No, I hadn't."

"And you don't know whether or not the children had said anything to Mr. Walsh?"

"No."

"Did you ever hear Mrs. Walsh discussing this relationship?"

"No."

John Blanchard, the assistant prosecuting attorney, asked Ruth if she remembered making certain statements to the state police on the day of the murder. In one statement she quoted Angus as telling her "something about his marriage vows, saying 'Until death do us part,' and that his wife was making him part, and he just couldn't stand it."

Under recross-examination by Mr. Salim, Ruth was asked, "In connection with your statement that you heard him say, 'In our marriage vows, it said, "Until death do us part," and she was making us part,' didn't you think that was rather odd to hear a man say this? Didn't that strike you as being strange as a reason for the killing?"

"I didn't think of it as the reason for the killing," she said. "I was just thinking that he was recalling what they had said in their marriage vows."

"Did he appear to be flippant or sincere in his statement?"

"I would say he was sincere."

"Like he really believed 'Until death do us part'?"

"Yes," she said.

The state trooper who had arrested Angus also took the stand. He described how, when he had pulled up to the address he was given, which was the Smith home, he saw a man and woman standing in the driveway. The man said, "I just shot my wife," and the woman said, "He just killed his wife."

The trooper then told the man to get into the car and drove him across the highway to his house. On the way, the trooper asked, "Are you sure she's dead?" explaining to the court that he wanted to know what to expect when he arrived at the house, whether to take in first-aid equipment. Angus told him, "I'm sure. I shot her six times in the head."

The trooper testified, "I asked, 'With what?' And he said, 'The same thing you've got there,' pointing to my gun at my side. Making a gesture toward my gun. He said a .357 Magnum 'with hunting loads, and you know what they'll do.' Then we went into the house."

He described Mrs. Walsh as "still sitting in the chair at the end of the table; she appeared quite dead. She had a number of visible wounds to her face and head, from what looked like gunshot wounds. And there was a large quantity of blood and bone fragments on the floor." He took Angus out to the patrol car, advised him he was under arrest and read him his rights. He asked Angus if he wished to have a lawyer, and Angus replied he did not need one.

"And then I asked him what had happened up to this point of the shooting," said the trooper. "He started to say that it was too much to tell. He said, 'Actually it began twelve years ago when we got married.' And he said they had been having trouble all through the twelve years. He said his dad had advised him not to marry the girl. And they hadn't got along too well since."

Angus told him about being served with the divorce papers, "and then he said that she didn't know it, but that was her obituary."

Angus also told him how he had begged his mother-in-law to take Ellen with her, how he went upstairs to get his suitcase, putting the gun in it "because he didn't want the children to see it and be afraid of it." He said that when he walked over to his wife and pointed the gun at her, "he was trying to scare her out of sending him away. He said she pushed the gun away. He brought it back and pointed it at her temple and shot her. He said he thought at this time that he didn't want any half job. And he shot her five more times. . . . He said he didn't think the children had seen the incident. He did say that he thought one of the girls had run up to the back door after the shooting."

The trooper also recalled that in questioning Angus, Angus had told him "he had just paid off all of his indebtedness and that he owned the house, and everything that was there he owned free and clear." He also quoted Angus as referring to the divorce papers, "saying something to the effect that it was her death warrant, the papers being served upon him."

The trooper also remembered that Angus had told him that one of the reasons for quarreling with his wife was that "she seemed to think he spent too much time hunting and being involved with his shooting and hunting rather than being with her and the family."

He described Angus as cooperative, not in any respect argumentative, and submissive when asked to put on handcuffs. Asked if Angus displayed emotion, the trooper said, "He would shake his head every now and then, put his head down and mumble something, and then he would come out with a statement."

He told how Angus walked over to where his dead wife was still sitting, leaned down, kissed her on the neck, and said, "It doesn't matter, but I still love you."

Mr. Salim asked, "Didn't you think it was unusual for a man to do that?"

"I don't know," said the trooper.

"Didn't you think what he did was unusual—to go over and kiss a lady who had been shot in the face five or six times, blood all over her, and say something to her?"

Said the trooper, "It would be unusual for me, but whether for him, I didn't know."

Mr. Blanchard asked the judge to bind the matter over to Circuit Court on the charge of first degree murder. Mr. Salim presented the psychiatric report, pleading insanity at the time of the committing of the murder. The judge ruled second degree murder and ordered Angus committed to a state mental hospital.

He remained there two years, then was discharged and returned to work. His children live with their maternal grandparents.

❧❧❧❧❧❧❧❧

This case shows how the insanity defense, in spite of all the hysterical propaganda against it, can be of great social significance. A man like Angus Walsh would no doubt have been convicted of first degree murder and sentenced to life in prison without this particular legal device. This is also one instance that clearly shows how the presence of a gun at the scene of a quarrel led to a murder that otherwise probably would not have occurred.

Here a husband murdered his wife rather than be parted from her. We do not know enough about Angus's boyhood to discuss specific childhood experiences in relation to his later ones. But when an adult kills rather than give up another adult he loves, he is caught in the fantasy of childhood that he and his mother are one, that his mother belongs to him and must never leave him. Ellen took the place of the mother from whom Angus had never been able to separate emotionally.

Probably the greatest number of so-called "crimes of passion" occur when someone who has been close threatens to desert or does desert the one to whom he has been close. Why is the threat of abandonment so devastating to some people that they will kill the one who has made the threat? It is as though the crime of abandonment is so obscene that it must be punished by death.

To a child, the greatest crime his mother can commit is to abandon him or threaten to abandon him, for then he will die. There will be no one to care for him or to love him, and he will lose all identity. The panic of a child whose mother threatens to walk out and leave him feeling unloved, unwanted, worthless, is repeated every time this child, as an adult, hears the same threat from someone he loves.

Usually the child who has the kind of mother who threatens

to leave him, as an adult will seek a mate who is the same kind of person, one who threatens to desert. Also, the intensity of panic in a child is stronger if he has a mother who threatens to abandon him, though all children to a certain degree fear separation from the mother and gradually have to learn to trust themselves to survive alone.

The abandonment by a mother does not even have to be a literal one. A child will feel deserted if he has a mother who pays him an inordinate amount of attention as a baby, then for some reason neglects him, either because another child is born, or the child himself has become older and starts to oppose her, or her husband has left her and she becomes depressed. A mother may also pay too much attention to a child, making it difficult for him to separate from her psychologically, and the very thought of separation from someone to whom he has become intensely attached will send him into panic as an adult.

We can speculate that Angus as a child felt that if his mother abandoned him he could not live. He never felt confidence in himself as a man; we know he was sexually inadequate in the sense he could not give affection or tenderness. He talked of sex as "a job." He said he was lucky if he "got it" once a week at the start. He thought of sex not as an act in which two persons give each other pleasure but as an act in which one person "gets" something from the other. He treated his wife as an inanimate object, there only to service him. He sometimes called her "the woman," thus taking all identity from her. He compared his love for her, in the interview with me, with love for a dog, and she must at times have felt treated as a dog. Also, knowing that if she became pregnant she faced another Caesarean section, she must have dreaded sex with him.

He kept saying his wife was trying to "destroy" him and "everything" he had built up. He felt her desire to seek divorce as castration. To him it meant she was denying that he was a man, as she had accused him of not being sexual. She had said to him, "All you want to do is roll me over and do it." There was no tenderness, no foreplay in their sex; she never had the feeling of being loved.

Angus said of the murder that he "had to do it, like I was being told I had to do it." This is how people feel when they are driven by unconscious impulses over which they have no control. In times of great stress, the unconscious will take over, overpowering all reason.

Angus must have realized that his wife was having affairs with other men. The children knew, and it is almost impossible to keep children from telling one parent all about the misbehavior of the other parent. But he closed his eyes to all thoughts of her infidelity, denying the possibility, saying, "I just couldn't make myself believe it" when she told him she no longer loved him. He thought, with the egomania of a child, that this could not be, she could not possibly love anyone else.

When she abandoned him, she destroyed him, he believed. The first reaction to abandonment is fury; then follows grief. Angus had for his wife the fierce possessive love of a child for a mother. He could not allow his loved one to have feelings of her own. Nor could he allow her to leave him. She belonged to him—until death did them part. No other man would ever have her. He made sure of that.

Early in 1976 I had occasion to speak to Angus Walsh's lawyer, who told me that Angus, who was living in northern Michigan, appeared to be getting along well. My wife Sandy and our four-year-old son David were heading for a vacation in that area, so I picked up the phone and called Angus. I told him we would like to stop and see him. He sounded pleased.

As we approached his home, I thought how accurately he had described it to me. Opposite his house stood the home of the neighbors, from which he had called the police after shooting his wife. The two houses were located in a scenic setting of woods. Angus's home had a picture-postcard quality. An American flag flew in front of it, and a large stone eagle perched on the side lawn.

Angus came to the door looking unchanged. The interior of the house was neat and clean, and Sandy, who in my opinion is an expert homemaker, commented to Angus, "I think I could take lessons in housekeeping from you."

He was pleased with her compliment. He showed us around and served coffee cake he had baked himself. I noticed large binoculars on a tripod, and he said he used them to watch for deer and other animals behind his home and in the nearby woods. He still continued to hunt and keep guns around. A pair of antique pistols was mounted over the fireplace.

We did not discuss much about his past. He mentioned that he was not allowed to see his children, that they had been completely turned against him by his late wife's parents. He said he had tried to fight the parents but was advised against it. I told him that he should vigorously pursue visitation rights, that his children should know they had been deprived of contact with him not because of his lack of interest in them but because of their grandparents' stand. He was obviously hurt by the fact that the children had a hostile attitude toward him.

As he showed us the children's bedrooms, he displayed little emotion until when we came to his son's bedroom, in which a model train track and other toys were left untouched. As he encouraged my son to play with the toys, his eyes filled with tears; he was clearly overcome by his feelings. I commented that the room was too cold for David to play in, for Angus did not heat the vacant bedrooms, and this gave us all a good excuse to go downstairs. He also showed us a pool table he kept in his recreation room in the basement and gave David and me our first instructions in pool. We also played ping-pong. He told me he had continued to work at the plant, where he had received regular promotions.

I observed how gentle and patient he was with David. I thought how deeply he missed his children. This was the real punishment for his moment of temporary madness, a punishment that would last the rest of his life.

5

"The Only Woman I Ever Loved"

It started with a telephone call in the summer of 1962.

My secretary buzzed my office and said, "A lawyer named Sheldon Otis wants to talk to you."

"Okay."

A patient had cancelled, and I was preparing notes for my class at Wayne State University Medical School, where I taught psychiatry to medical students. This was early in my career as a courtroom psychiatrist, and I presumed Mr. Otis, as several other lawyers had done, wanted to ask some legal-psychiatric question.

A pleasant, masculine voice said over the telephone, "Thank you for talking to me, Dr. Tanay. Supreme Court Justice Theodore Souris referred me to you. I'm his legal assistant." Judge Souris was a member of the State Supreme Court of Michigan.

Mr. Otis explained further, "I'm defending a client against a murder charge. His name is Fred Lane. You probably read about him in the papers a few months ago. They referred to him as 'the mercy killer.' "

"I remember reading about him," I said.

"He strangled a woman with whom he'd been living when

she had a very severe asthmatic attack. Then he tried to commit suicide by putting a plastic bag over his head and lying down on the bed beside her."

"Why are you calling me?" I asked, though I could make a good guess as to the reason.

"To ask if you would examine Mr. Lane and testify at his trial as to possible temporary insanity at the time he committed the murder."

I said thoughtfully, "I must warn you I have a long-standing aversion to appearing in court. I don't think psychiatrists do much good in a courtroom. Judges and prosecutors are out to make fools of them."

The judicial process, as far as I was concerned, could stick to its own psychiatric experts, some of whom I had heard accused of selling their services to the highest bidder. A psychiatrist in private practice had no place in a courtroom, I believed. I thought I knew better than to allow myself to testify in court, though I had done it once against my better judgment. But Mr. Otis was challenging my intellectual curiosity. It might be an interesting experience. Perhaps in some small way I might even be able to influence the law to consider a more rational definition of insanity, though, I thought ironically, I had such strong feelings about the McNaughton rule that I might wind up in jail for contempt of court.

In this country legal insanity is determined by the McNaughton rule, also called the right and wrong test. The question is: Can the murderer distinguish right from wrong at the time he commits the act? The answer has to be either yes or no. If he can distinguish right from wrong, he is guilty and has to go to prison. If he cannot, he can be judged insane and sent to a mental institution. I could hear the judge order, "Answer yes or no—could Mr. Lane distinguish right from wrong at the time he committed the act?" And I could hear myself insisting, "I cannot give a yes or no answer. It is not that simple." Whereupon I would be hauled away, and the next day my photograph would appear in the papers under the heading "Psychiatrist Jailed for Contempt of Court."

In addition to my strong feelings about the uselessness of testifying in court, I was loath to cancel appointments with patients. Every cancelled or missed appointment causes conscious and unconscious grief and anger in a patient.

And yet one thing fascinated me as a psychiatrist. I was intrigued with the element of "no air," the feeling of suffocation, that pervaded the Lane case: the attack of asthma, the strangling, the attempted suicide via a plastic bag. This theme of suffocation, perhaps psychological as well as physical—can one ever separate the two?—appealed to the psychic detective in me.

Mr. Otis was asking, "Would you consider examining Mr. Lane?"

I hesitated, then said, "I don't know." My response was honest, though evasive, showing my ambivalence.

Then I realized how unfair this was to Mr. Otis. I added, as though to rationalize my feelings, "Your client does not sound overtly mentally ill. If I see him and believe no psychiatric disorder is present, then you have done him a disservice, because even if I don't appear in court, the prosecution may ask you my findings, and you will have to say they were not favorable to your client."

"I realize this," said Mr. Otis. "It's a danger that confronts a lawyer every time he asks a psychiatrist whose opinion he does not know in advance to examine his client."

Now it was Mr. Otis's turn to be silent, as though he were thinking what to do next.

I suggested, "Why don't you think it over before authorizing me to see your client?"

I had become acquainted with at least that much of the law to know that a lawyer's job is to defend his client rather than search for the truth. That was why I asked Mr. Otis to think over whether he wanted me to testify in court.

He said, "Thank you for discussing this with me. I'll get back to you shortly," and hung up.

❖❖❖❖❖❖❖

Five days later Mr. Otis called back. He said, "I've decided to take the risk of having you examine my client and testify in court. Will you see him as soon as possible? He's being held in Wayne County Jail."

Cancelling patients for the day of July 8, 1962, I traveled to Wayne County Jail. It is a dismal, depressing architectural monstrosity, resembling most of the nation's jails. I had visited it before, and once again I experienced that feeling of oppressive collective guilt at permitting such unholy habitations to exist, one of society's crimes against those who, though accused of a crime, have not yet been convicted and may be innocent.

My first impression of Fred Lane, as we met in the visitors' room, was of a mild-mannered, passive, friendly man, of average height and average build. Bushy white hair gave him a striking appearance, rather like Santa Claus. His smile was warm, his handshake firm.

He spoke straightforwardly and simply, answering my questions directly. He told me that he had been raised by his mother, that he had never known his father, that before he was born, his father had left for Europe. Fred Lane had had two older sisters, one of whom he described as old enough "to be my mother." His mother, his two sisters, and he had lived in Chicago until 1915, then, when he was twelve, went to Detroit. He had lived with his mother until her death in 1928 after a long illness during which he took care of her.

Though his mother had left him her small house, he gave it to his sister and lived there with her. "I was like a boarder," he said. He maintained the same dependent relationship to his sister as he had to his mother. During the depression of the 1930s he lost the house, and his sister went on welfare. She died in 1943, but prior to her death she was ill, and he took care of her just as he had his mother. Following his sister's death, he moved to the YMCA and lived there for twelve years. He occasionally saw his other sister and her son, and a few friends with whom he played cards and bowled.

Then in 1955, when he was fifty-two years old, he met Maggie Brant, a widow with a married daughter. He told me, "Maggie was the only woman I ever loved." He lived with her on and off for seven years. They went everywhere as man and wife. Even her daughter believed they were married. They did not marry, he explained, because the money she was receiving from the pension of her late husband would have been cut off.

From the day he met her, she suffered from asthma, and it

was always a source of difficulty for them. One time they were forced to move from a rooming house because the landlady complained that her husband could not stand Maggie's constant coughing. In the spring of 1961, he and Maggie separated for a while after a quarrel. He left for Chicago. After a few months he returned to Detroit. Maggie found him and begged him to come back to her, which he did.

He spoke of himself as having always felt lonely, accustomed to doing things on his own. He said he tried to be nice to everyone, never expressed anger. He had never been involved in any trouble with the law. He had always been responsible and honest in his work. He had held one job in a plastics factory for twenty-one years, but since 1960, two years before the "mercy killing," he had been unable to get regular employment. He had tried one job in a gas station, but after working two hours he had slipped in a pool of grease and broken his leg, and was taken to Detroit Receiving Hospital. Since then, he had found it impossible to get any kind of work and had to ask his nephew occasionally for small sums of money.

It was clear that Mr. Lane had felt just as dependent on and attached to Maggie as he had to his mother and, later, to his sister. He gave me a detailed account of Maggie's long asthmatic illness, recalling frequent attacks for which she was regularly treated at doctors' offices and in hospitals. I got the impression that their entire life centered on the treatment of her asthmatic attacks. Whatever money they received would be spent for medication and medicinal sprays, or gas for the car so they could visit doctors and hospitals. He frequently had to borrow money from relatives and friends to pay for the medication and for bills incurred in emergency rooms of hospitals. He said that prior to the killing he had given his last eight dollars to a doctor to help Maggie through an attack.

He went over the circumstances of the crime itself several times, each time telling the same story. In substance, this is what he said had occurred early in the morning of March 13, 1962:

He had been listening through the night, as he had so many nights, over so many years, to Maggie's asthmatic choking. Sometimes he thought she would choke to death before he could

reach her side and give her the medication or spray that miracul-
ously allowed her to breathe in precious air once more.

He had been up all that night. She had had a severe attack
about midnight, and he had warmed milk on a hotplate which the
landlady had given them. She seemed better after drinking the
milk, and he lay down beside her, trying not to move so he would
not disturb her. He was too upset to fall asleep.

A few hours later she started to have another attack. Her
breath came in rasping, anguished gasps. He looked at the clock
on the table beside the double bed and saw that it was almost 3
A.M.

This was Tuesday. They had run out of medication on Friday. There was no money left in the rented room, and he had
driven to the hospital to try to sell his blood to a blood bank, but
they turned him down because his blood type was wrong.

On Saturday he had gone to Maggie's daughter to ask for
money. He told her that they had sold everything they owned and
that her mother was so helpless he had to comb her hair for her.
Maggie's daughter gave him five dollars, saying that was all she
could spare, and with it he bought medicinal spray. That day he
also managed to borrow ten dollars from a neighbor and bought
gas to drive Maggie to Saratoga Hospital, where they gave her
medication.

She had seemed better Saturday night, even slept for hours
without an attack. But on Monday she was worse. She began
spitting blood. He knew she belonged in a hospital. At least he
should take her to a doctor. But there was no money to pay for a
doctor.

When she suffered the second asthmatic attack at 3 A.M., he
again got out of bed and warmed what was left of the milk and
gave it to her. But she kept spitting blood. He thought it must be a
very bad attack. He wiped her perspiring face, trying to comfort
her.

Then he took a towel to wipe Maggie's saliva and spit off his
own hands. As he sat on the edge of the bed, holding the towel,
he noticed lying on the floor the newspaper of the day before. He
picked it up and read a story about a boy who had killed his
parents and brother and sister. When asked why, the boy had

given as his reason for murder that they would no longer "have to suffer."

He sat clutching the towel. Maggie was again wheezing, again in anguish, again suffering, as she had suffered for seven years with him by her side.

Suddenly his hands tightened on the towel. He made a knot in it. He stood up and moved toward Maggie's side of the bed. He moved closer and closer to Maggie's gray head, her open, choking mouth. He leaned over her. Her eyes were closed in pain, her face almost blue.

He slipped the knotted towel around her neck, the knot against her windpipe. He pulled it tight. Tighter. Tighter still. She struggled against his pull. She cried out, "Fred, don't!" He drowned out her cries by putting a pillow over her face.

Then all at once she gave up the struggle. Her body fell off the bed to the floor. He picked her up—she wasn't very heavy, about one hundred pounds—and put her back on the bed. Her tongue protruded from her mouth, and he pushed it back in. He folded her hands as though she were praying and kissed her on the cheek. Then he lay down by her side, feeling peaceful for the first time in days.

But the peace did not last long. He rose, went to the bureau, took a plastic bag out of the drawer. He put it over his head, then lay down again next to Maggie, thinking he would choke to death. But nothing happened.

After a few minutes he got up, took off his pajamas, put on his only suit. It was now eight o'clock. His nephew would be getting up to go to work.

He left the room in which Maggie and he had lived together, walked out of the house and climbed into his car. He drove to his nephew's house, parked the car, walked up to the front door and knocked. His nephew opened the door, a look of surprise on his face at this early-morning visit.

Fred Lane told his nephew what he had done, tears in his eyes. He said, "I'm giving you title to my car. I won't need a car where I'm going."

His nephew drove him to the Highland Park Police Station. As they walked into the station, the sergeant on duty was working on a crossword puzzle. Fred Lane said to the sergeant, "I want to report a murder. I just killed my wife."

The sergeant put down the crossword puzzle.

✧✧✧✧✧✧✧✧

After interviewing Fred Lane, I had a conference with Mr. Otis. I told him, "I believe Mr. Lane suffered from a sudden, overwhelming dissociative reaction that rendered him incapable of controlling his impulse to kill."

Mr. Otis looked at me thoughtfully, then said, "Do you know how difficult it will be to convince a jury that a man who was otherwise normal, at least who will be normal at the time of the trial, was, on that particular morning, suddenly unable to control his impulse to kill?"

"I know," I said. "That's one reason I've been reluctant to appear in courtrooms."

He warned, "The jury is not composed of Ph.D.s. You'll have to state your concepts very simply."

"I'll do my best," I said.

We discussed several issues in detail. For the first time I realized the extensive preparation a lawyer must invest in a case before he even steps into the courtroom—for example, in the selection of jurors. The lawyer has the choice of rejecting a juror if he feels that juror is prejudiced. The question arose as to whether a juror who had someone in his family suffering from asthma, who might, like Fred Lane, have had to stay up nights caring for an asthmatic patient, would be more understanding and sympathetic. I advised Mr. Otis against accepting such a juror, for I believed he would not be more sympathetic. He might be struggling against his own negative feelings toward the asthmatic member of his family. He might more easily condemn someone like Fred Lane, who had given vent to feelings the juror found unacceptable to his own self-image.

The trial was scheduled for Monday, September 10, 1962. As it turned out, I was not to appear until Wednesday. I had intended to be in court during the initial testimony of other witnesses and the defendant, but I was informed I was not allowed in the courtroom, that prospective witnesses were excluded.

I was to be the first witness on Wednesday morning, to explain the issue of temporary insanity, one that has puzzled and fascinated lawyers and judges, not to mention psychiatrists, over the centuries. While waiting for court to be declared in session, as a newcomer to the scene I studied everyone involved. First and foremost, I was impressed with the change that had occurred in Mr. Otis. When I first saw him, he seemed a calm, relaxed, easygoing and attentive young man. But now he was quite tense and intense, fully absorbed by the trial and constantly anticipating new developments. He was clearly responsible for carrying the burden for our side. His assistant was Mrs. Jane Souris, the wife of Supreme Court Justice Souris, who is now a successful practicing attorney but then was a law student. She sat next to Mr. Otis, prepared to take careful notes on the proceedings, for it was important for us to know which cards were played and how by the prosecution. She was our final authority as to who said what, such as, "Did Mr. Lane say the towel was on the bed, or did he say it was on the chair?" As I soon discovered when I got on the stand, it was not important what I knew but only what already was in the record. Even if some fact, in my opinion, was very well established, if it was not part of the record, I could not use it.

Mr. Lane was dressed up and looked more conventional than he had in the county jail. He had that certain "just like you and me" look, and I hoped this would have a good effect on the jury, the members of whom all seemed to be fully aware of their responsibility as they exhibited a collective, inscrutable poker face. Mrs. Souris and Mr. Otis were proud of "their" jury, and I thought they had good reason to be inasmuch as the members all looked fairly young and intelligent. The judge, who was quite young, seemed pleasant and intelligent.

The prosecutor was a surprise to me. He did not have the lean and hungry look I associated with the stereotyped prosecutor. He appeared quite well fed and friendly. The courtroom was full. I recognized several familiar faces, including a resident from my service at Detroit Receiving Hospital and a few medical students from the class I taught at Wayne State University Medical School. I was also informed some legal students were present.

I was duly sworn in, and my day in court began. First, there was direct examination by the defense counsel, Mr. Otis, who demonstrated, through asking me questions, that I was "eminently qualified," to use his phrase. We discussed in an interchange of questions and answers my medical training, hospital residency, teaching, appointments, administrative experience, and papers presented at society meetings. The fact that I was an assistant professor was brought out, as well as the fact that I was qualified by the American Board of Psychiatry and Neurology in the specialty of psychiatry. The jury also learned that I would not be making much money in testifying, that the fee would be up to the court. I was asked if I expected a higher fee if the case were decided in our favor, a question most distasteful to me, but one Mr. Otis felt important. The answer, of course, was no.

Then Mr. Otis asked me what diagnosis, if any, I had made as a result of my examination of Fred Lane.

I replied, "I made the diagnosis of dissociative reaction."

"What, Doctor, is dissociative reaction?" he asked.

"This is a disease of the mind that is characterized by the person's being overwhelmed. Psychiatrists would call it disruption of one's ego."

"Doctor, what, if any, additional diagnosis did you make at the completion of your examination?" Mr. Otis asked.

"I felt there were a number of predisposing factors in Mr. Lane's case. One was the fact that he suffers from a rather weak ego. Another was that at the time the act occurred he was under extreme tension that was a result of his identification with a particular person, namely Mrs. Brant." I also said that Mr. Lane could not control or resist the impulse to kill Maggie Brant.

"Doctor, can you explain for us the basis for that opinion?" asked Mr. Otis.

"At the time the event occurred, he was overwhelmed and entered the state I previously mentioned—dissociative reaction. It means that the controlling part of his personality, his ego, was no longer functioning, and he was responding like an automaton. In other words, there was a stimulus and there was an immediate response, whereas the essence of being a normal adult is that if there is some stimulus, there is some thought, some ego activity, as we call it, interposed between the impulse and the action.

"In Mr. Lane's circumstance, there was no such interposing delay. Impulse and act occurred just like an automatic mechanism. Here was the towel, here was the choking woman, and he acted as if he were controlled by external force. There are many other instances of similar behavior. For example, a soldier who is overwhelmed by anxiety in the front lines suddenly begins to run and gets shot. Although it makes no sense, he could no longer control his impulse to run, though if he had remained stationary, he would have lived.''

I said that the stress that precipitated Mr. Lane's act in this situation "was his identification with the suffering woman. It seemed to be happening to him in a sense. I think we are all familiar with this feeling.

"Let's say two factory workers work side by side. One gets his finger cut off. The other suddenly experiences pain in that same finger. This is what we call identification. If a child cries, his mother responds with discomfort and does something to stop the child from crying. We know of cases where parents have killed their children because the children did not stop crying. They become identified with the suffering child.''

Mr. Otis, bringing out the background of Fred Lane, asked, "Doctor, is there any particular psychiatric significance to the fact that this man did not know who his father was?''

I replied, "I think there was significance in that. As I previously mentioned, I feel this man had a very weak ego because he grew up in very impoverished circumstances. He did not have a father. His subsequent life also indicated he always needed someone to lean upon. He always needed a crutch. First it was the mother with whom he lived. Then it was a sister with whom he lived. Then it was Maggie. He could never quite function on his own. The weaker the ego, the easier it is for it to become overwhelmed by some external or internal stress or stimulus. It is just like a fuse. The lower the fuse, the easier it is for it to blow under stress or under an overload of electricity.''

"And, Doctor, is there any psychiatric significance to the fact that he had not married or did not have a marriage relationship until he was over the age of fifty?''

"Yes. This further confirms that he was a very passive, a very dependent individual. As long as he could live with his mother or his sister, he was like a little boy. When these people died, he had to seek out some other crutch. He could never really function on his own.''

"Doctor, is there any psychiatric significance to the fact concerning the efforts of this man to help Maggie by trying to sell his blood to get her medical care and attention, and other ways in which he attended to her?"

"Yes. I think he was again trying to relieve a state of tension, as a mother tries to pacify a child because it makes her uncomfortable when the child cries. He was trying to do everything in his power to stop Maggie from suffering, because the suffering was almost happening to him in his mind."

"Doctor, can you tell us what, if any, psychiatric significance there is to the fact concerning the newspaper article which has been described, and the absence of relief for the asthmatic attack on the night this incident occurred?"

"When this incident occurred, it was, as I said, a kind of automatic response. There was the stimulus of the towel. On the floor lay the paper from the night or the day before, with a story of a boy who killed to relieve his parents' suffering, and there was the choking woman, and all of this in an instant became interconnected in one action designed to relieve his state of tension."

"Doctor, is there any significance to the facts concerning his attempt to take his own life with the plastic bag by attempting to choke off his own breath?"

"Yes. Psychiatrically, this confirms the fact he was trying to be one with her, that he lay down by her side and was not excited. Anyone who commits such an act would normally become very excited. If you run over somebody or hurt somebody, you become distressed and anxious, whereas this man's reaction was of relaxation. Before this point, he was distressed. The moment the act was committed, he was able to lie next to her, put his arms around her as if everything were nice and peaceful once again."

"And did this act serve any function for him?"

"I think it reestablished the relationship that existed when she wasn't suffering. It relieved something within him. He was not aiming at affecting her in any way. It was happening to him, and once he got rid of his tension, he was able to lie down and be more comfortable, in a sense."

"What significance do you attach to the fact of his getting dressed, going to his nephew and then to the police, and telling his story?"

"It is the same continuing action that I just finished talking about. He wasn't excited. He wasn't agitated. He went as a man who has just relieved himself of unbearable tension. Now he could go ahead and do things the usual way, though up to this point he wasn't quite himself, as I mentioned."

"Doctor, what disease of the mind did you describe this man as possessing?"

"Dissociative reaction, which is a response to an overwhelming stress. Psychiatry has recently proven that every human being is susceptible to this. For example, research done for the purpose of space flight has shown that under a great deal of stimulus any human being reaches a point where his ego will fail. This was proved in isolation experiments. Also, during World War II, a great deal of information was accumulated about the reaction of soldiers to overwhelming stress. They would enter a state of consciousness where they had no control over their actions, although otherwise they were normal."

"And as a result of this state, you say this man could not control the impulse to commit the act? He couldn't resist the impulse?"

"The impulse bypassed all conscious control. As I said, it was a kind of automatic reaction, just as you would respond to a reflex when you no longer have conscious control of what you are doing. Or as you commit an act in your sleep. Your ego, your control agency, is asleep in the dissociative state, as in sleep."

Mr. Otis asked what psychiatric significance I attached to the fact that the murder was committed after a long night of suffering and that no one else had been present in the room.

"I think that is very important," I said. "The stress of the preceding days was another factor that weakened this man's already weak ego. We know very well, for example, that the ego control of a pilot who has been under a great deal of stress is not as good as a pilot who has rested. Mr. Lane was up for a few nights taking care of Maggie Brant. There was no one around, and even the time of night contributed to the situation, one of the many facts that resulted in this one explosion, in his being overwhelmed by tension."

This concluded Mr. Otis's questions for the time being. I felt I had talked freely, as if in a classroom. I had to make the jury understand the nature of Mr. Lane's mental illness. If they did not, I could not shift the blame onto anyone else.

Then followed my cross-examination by the prosecuting attorney. First he undertook to undermine my "eminent qualifications." He juggled a few dates in the hope of making me appear inconsistent. He stressed my lack of experience in giving testimony in court—I had testified only once before in a murder trial, in 1954 in Illinois. He asked questions about Mr. Lane, and I answered, always trying to get across my message—that he was suffering from a disease called "dissociative reaction."

The prosecutor tried to show that dissociative reaction was not a psychosis and therefore not a mental disease. The drift of his questions seemed to suggest that dissociative reaction was some rare bird I had discovered, or possibly invented, which had little if anything to do with the beast known as mental illness. I knew that the legal requirement for insanity was that the act of murder was an expression and manifestation of the diseased mind. There had to be a "disease"; then came the impulse that was "irresistible." If this implication was not upheld, we did not have a case.

He asked if I had had occasion to treat or diagnose other persons with dissociative reactions. I indicated that since I had been involved in the case of Mr. Lane, I had become aware of quite a few homicides involving spouses that were of the same nature. The prosecutor emphasized this point, then a recess was called. Mr. Otis commented to me that my last answer had created a bad impression on the jury because it sounded as if Mr. Lane's act had started an epidemic of murder of spouses, and that therefore his punishment would be a social necessity as a deterrent to future homicides. I thought this an ironic footnote to the pitfalls of psychiatric testimony in the courts.

After the recess, the prosecutor asked the court reporter to read the last sentences of the testimony, so the jury had the opportunity to hear the passage a second time. Later I attempted to clarify the point, so they heard it a third time. The prosecutor then continued to dissect my testimony. He pointed out that Mr. Lane was sane after the act and evidently quite sane until the act, and asked when the "mysterious disease" had taken possession of him. The prosecutor did not state this clearly but implied that Mr. Lane's illness and his act of murder were one and the same. It sounded as if he were saying that what the man in the street calls murder the psychiatrist calls dissociative reaction.

Then we had a little encounter over the McNaughton rule.

The prosecutor said, "I would assume, Doctor, that you are familiar with the distinction between legal insanity, medical insanity, and insanity as the layman might normally view it?"

"I prefer not to use the term 'insanity,' because, in my opinion, it is strictly a legal term, just as, for example, 'murder' is strictly a legal term and we don't use it medically," I said. "Our textbooks never use a term like insanity."

He asked what treatment I prescribed for "mental disease" of a "dissociative reaction."

I said, "The treatment consists of long-term psychotherapy. However, in a situation where a man is present for evaluation only, no specific treatment was prescribed or was possible."

Then he asked if the dissociative reaction came from over-worry or overwork.

I replied, "No, from being overwhelmed by some external or internal stimulation."

"Is this dissociative reaction, Doctor, a temporary diseased condition, or is it a diseased condition which may have existed over a period of years?"

"The predisposition to it is something that exists over the years. The acute symptoms of it usually are much more short-lived," I replied.

The question as to whether Fred Lane was able to distinguish between right and wrong remained up in the air. The prosecutor asked whether Mr. Lane was conscious of what he was doing and, if he was conscious, if his perception was intact, his ego intact, since perception was a function of the ego. His questions were quite skillful and consistent, but I felt I held my own. I kept repeating that Fred Lane had no conscious control, that his ego was overwhelmed because of the tension created by his identification with the suffering woman, that the pain of the suffering woman became his own, and this caused a loss of consciousness, just as a person faints when he experiences too much pain.

Then Mr. Otis had a chance at redirect examination. He asked if I was the one who originally described the diagnosis of dissociative reaction. This gave me a chance to elaborate upon the fact that it was a well-established identity. I quoted as authority the Diagnostic Manual of the American Psychiatric Association.

The second question Mr. Otis directed to me was quite

informative. He asked if I would have been able to give my testimony without having personally examined the defendant, hinting the prosecution might be calling a witness who had done just that. I searched the courtroom for another psychiatrist who might testify for the prosecution. Up to now, Mr. Lane had not been examined by the prosecution, and there had been no indication they planned to introduce an expert of their own. But this question from Mr. Otis was a subtle announcement to me that a so-called battle of the experts was about to begin.

I answered his question with a supposedly innocent question of my own: "You mean like giving a diagnosis on the phone?" Then I made some remarks about the difficulties and the unreliability of formulations based on history only, without a personal interview.

Then came recess for lunch. Mr. Otis, Mrs. Souris, Mr. Lane, and I rushed into a little room off the corridor for a quick conference. We had been told the prosecution was bringing in its own psychiatric expert, Dr. William E. Gordon, and that he had asked to examine Mr. Lane during the lunch recess. Mr. Otis had the privilege of giving or denying permission for such an examination. If he refused, the prosecution could not tell the jury that permission had been denied.

I believed Mr. Otis should not permit the examination, that no good could come of it, and nothing was lost by refusing. Mr. Otis thought it over and decided to deny permission. We went to lunch at a restaurant full of lawyers, most of whom knew Mr. Otis and all about the trial and freely gave advice. There was general concern about Dr. Gordon, who seemed well known to the other lawyers. Several warned us that he would distort the facts and unless we had on-the-spot evidence to disprove what he said, we would be in trouble. We speculated about the approach he might take. Mr. Otis appeared anxious, foresaw all kinds of complications. In the years to come, Dr. Gordon and I were to cross swords many times in courtrooms. He was regularly called by the prosecution. On the few occasions when I was aware he was called by the defense, he usually gave a response contrary to the defense attorney's expectation. In at least one such case, he examined the accused man on behalf of the defense, then turned around and testified on behalf of the prosecution. In another case, that of a doctor who had killed his wife and four-year-old son, the prosecution anticipated the insanity defense and asked Dr. Gordon to examine the defendant almost immediately after the murders, at the police station. I was told Dr. Gordon was at the police station before the defendant was brought in and had not as yet been arraigned or informed of his rights.

Recess was over. Dr. Gordon took the stand. This time the prosecutor was the first to question, since Dr. Gordon was his witness. He brought out the "eminent qualifications" of his expert: medical school, residency, two years in the Air Force, certified by the American Board of Psychiatry and Neurology in 1957, in private practice, and last but not least, physician for the city of Detroit. I thought, How misleading, attaching importance to Dr. Gordon's work as city physician, for his office was a little cubbyhole in our hospital, manned by three telephone operators who sent out doctors to check on emergencies at three dollars a call daytime rate, five dollars nighttime. I was not impressed with the position of city physician. But then, I was not on the jury.

The prosecutor asked Dr. Gordon if he had examined Mr. Lane, and Dr. Gordon quickly sneaked in the fact that he had been denied permission—or at least attempted to sneak it in by saying, "I requested the permission." Mr. Otis promptly objected, as was his right, and the judge and the two opposing lawyers retired to the judge's chambers, after which the question was stricken from the record.

Dr. Gordon reached opposite conclusions from mine. He said Fred Lane was normal, that he had hated his deceased common-law wife, he no longer could lean upon her, no longer could use her as a crutch, and therefore had decided to get rid of her. Dr. Gordon maintained Fred Lane had executed the murder in an orderly way, tied a single knot in the towel, and this was proof of his conscious, deliberate intention to kill her. He suffered from no illness. Even assuming my diagnosis was correct, namely that he did have "dissociative reaction," he still suffered no disease. Dissociative reaction might be listed in the Diagnostic Manual of the American Psychiatric Association, but it was merely a symptom, not a disease.

Then Mr. Otis had to make the decision whether to put me on the witness stand as the so-called surrebuttal witness. He wondered if I could say anything new. Mr. Otis, Mrs. Souris, and I went into a quick huddle, and it was decided that I should take the stand again. Mrs. Souris said to me quietly but firmly, "You've got to make them believe."

When I was again on the stand, Mr. Otis asked questions, but he was too friendly and unable to tap the pent-up indignation within me. I felt that if only Dr. Gordon were standing in front of me, I would be able to answer with more fiery conviction.

But then the prosecutor began asking me questions. I knew this was the decisive moment. He said, "Dr. Tanay, according to your testimony, this dissociative reaction is universally, if I may use the term, known as a psychiatric disease with many symptoms, is that right?"

"Yes," I said.

"Now, you say that somnambulism is a symptom of dissociative reaction?"

"Yes."

"Do you call this a particular type of dissociative reaction, this somnambulism, or must there be something in addition before we have dissociative reaction, which you claim to be a recognized psychiatric disease?"

"A disease consists of a number of symptoms. For example, if you have heart disease, shortness of breath, and swollen legs, you don't have to have all the symptoms to be diagnosed as having 'congestive' failure. It's the same with dissociative reaction. The diagnosis is applied to someone who fulfills some of the criteria. He doesn't have to possess the whole list of them. In other words, a schizophrenic doesn't have to suffer from every possible schizophrenic symptom to be called a schizophrenic. If he has hallucinations and is delusional, that is enough to call him schizophrenic."

"Dr. Tanay, you testified you have had occasion to examine Fred Lane on numerous occasions, both at the Wayne County Jail and at Receiving Hospital."

"Yes."

"And you concluded that he was suffering from a dissociative reaction, which you define as a psychiatric disease?"

"Yes."

"Would you tell us then, please, Doctor, what symptoms you found in the defendant, Fred Lane, which led you to this conclusion?"

"I think I have stated them a number of times when referring to the history that I had of him and also his description of what happened at the time the act occurred, shortly prior to it and after it."

"Well, Dr. Tanay, during your examination of the defendant, did you find the symptom of somnambulism, sleepwalking? You didn't find this symptom, did you?"

"No, I didn't."

"You didn't find the symptom of a fugue state, did you?"

"You can list a half dozen things I didn't find."

"Well, Doctor, with your indulgence, perhaps I missed it, but would you restate for us the symptoms? Now, would you say that the history of this defendant was a symptom of the dissociative reaction?"

"History is not a symptom."

"Well, what were the symptoms that you found?"

"The symptoms were those of a man who has shown no propensity in his entire life to act out in any way or to commit criminal acts, and only under the distress of the situation that we have described, the unbearable things he was experiencing, did he commit a very irrational act. He killed a person he loved, although he had taken care of her for many, many months. He had a number of other opportunities when he could have taken her to Receiving Hospital and simply left her there. This is done every day. He could have solved the problem many other ways. Instead, he committed a very irrational act."

"Dr. Tanay, are you saying that by the very fact that this defendant, prior to this act, had led an entirely peaceful, law-abiding life, that the very commission of this act led you to believe that he suffered dissociative reaction?"

"Not the very commission of the act but the circumstances under which it occurred and the time and the manner."

"Would you then, Doctor, say that the explanation for the acts of the defendant under the circumstances outlined here would preclude a definite plan of action and a definite consciousness of the carrying out of that kind of action?"

"I would think so. I have an understanding of the case that I think I have presented here as to how it came about, and psychiatrically, to me, it is very clear what has occurred. Legally, it might not be as clear, but psychiatrically, I think there is no doubt that this man was in a state of dissociative reaction at the time."

"Would you, Doctor, entirely discount the application of the theory of the reverse dependency? You testified earlier, I believe, that this defendant, according to your examination, historically has been dependent, has needed a crutch, the first crutch being his mother, the second crutch being his sister, the last crutch being the deceased Maggie Brant, right?"

"Yes."

"Now, Doctor, do you entirely discount the theory that, because of the worsened condition of Maggie Brant, she no longer was the crutch upon which this defendant could lean, that there was a reverse situation as a result, that she became dependent on him, and as a result of that reverse dependency there was created in him a hostility which exploded on the morning of March 13, 1962?"

"Sir, I don't use terms that are not commonly used. In other words, I don't base my functioning in psychiatry upon something unknown. I do not stick to my own experience. You say reverse dependency, and I don't completely understand. It is completely unknown to me. I don't find—"

The prosecutor interrupted, "Let me explain it for you, Doctor, so you will understand what I am trying to say. You testified this defendant did need a crutch all his life?"

"Yes."

"He depended on his mother, and she died?"

"Yes."

"He lived with his sister, whom he depended on, and she died. He moved in with Maggie Brant and was dependent on her?"

"Yes."

"Now, dependency, Doctor, was your term?"

"Yes."

"Would you agree that when Maggie Brant became a chronic asthmatic she was no longer able to do those things for this defendant that his mother had done in the first instance, his sister had done in the second instance, and Maggie Brant had done in the initial stage of their relationship?"

"Yes."

"So then who becomes the crutch? Isn't it true that Maggie Brant no longer is a crutch but that the defendant becomes a crutch on which Maggie Brant must lean?"

"All right."

"Now, Doctor, we have a man who, according to your own testimony and according to your opinion, has had to have a crutch all of his life, and who suddenly finds himself in a position of being a crutch, and because he has been placed in this position, he creates within himself a hostility toward this person whom before he had depended on, and who now has become dependent on him. Is it possible, Doctor, that when that situation became apparent to the defendant, in order to wipe away the situation, it exploded in his hands on the morning of March 13, 1962? My question to you is, do you discard that possibility?"

"I do, because, you see, if you are referring to conscious intention and hostility, then it doesn't really make any kind of sense. If you say he may have unconscious hostility, he is not aware of this—after all, his history indicates he was willing to sell his blood to get help for her. If you say he resented her unconsciously and this resentment exploded on March 13 in his killing her, I would say yes. But if you say he consciously planned to get rid of her, there were many other steps he could have taken. He could have walked away and told her daughter, 'You take care of her, she's not my problem.' He could have left her on her own, and she would have died. He really was taking care of her. To walk away would be the rational act. But he committed an irrational act, so if he had any conscious hostility and was aware of it, he could have expressed it many, many other ways. He could have killed her and left her there, and nobody would have ever found out that he was the one who did it. How would they know? Here was a woman who had choked to death, known to everybody to be sick, a woman who was sixty years old. So, as a rational act, Mr. Lane's behavior makes absolutely no sense. As an irrational act, it does make sense."

As I answered Mr. Smith's questions, I felt that the witness chair had moved, that I was sitting in the jury box, talking only to the jury. I know I spoke loudly, even waving my hands at times. I was emotional, persuasive, even nasty at some points. Until I later read the transcript, I didn't recall what I had said. Fourteen years afterward, at a party, I overheard Jane Souris describing my testimony at that moment and the emotional response of the jury. Just recently she told me that the most dramatic moment in her entire courtroom career came as she listened to my last sentence: "As a rational act, it makes absolutely no sense; as an irrational act, it does make sense." Mass-murderer Charles Manson once echoed this idea when he said, "No sense makes sense," another way of saying that unconscious behavior makes sense if you understand the unconscious.

When the prosecutor finished with me, he asked for an adjournment, claiming laryngitis was getting the better of him. It was a shrewd move, since this was not the day to have the jury retire and deliberate. As I left the witness stand, people gathered around to congratulate me, as if I were an actor who had given a fine performance. Mr. Otis said with a broad smile, "You are developing into a real courtroom psychiatrist." I haven't as yet decided if this was a compliment. The prosecutor came over, shook my hand, congratulated me. This was my first awareness of a lawyer's ability to battle an opponent in court yet be friendly outside the courtroom.

As I made my way to the elevator, others approached me, expressing complimentary remarks. It was quite a day, and I felt confident that we had made our point.

The closing arguments took up the next day. I had two hours free from my practice and headed for the courtroom. In the elevator a young man from the prosecutor's office said, "You gave very good testimony. Too bad it won't do any good."

I asked, puzzled, "Why not?"

He replied, "Two opposing experts cancel each other out."

As I walked into the courtroom, I understood what he meant. The prosecutor was delivering his closing argument. He was repeating my testimony word for word. He was fair. He even called me a professor, graciously dropping the "assistant." He then repeated Dr. Gordon's testimony. He emphasized Dr. Gordon's qualifications and his experience in criminal matters, con-

trasting it with my lack of experience in testifying. He stressed
that we were both well qualified, reputable men, adding that even
well qualified experts did disagree.

He then exhorted the jury to be unemotional and decide the
case on legal grounds. His strategy was apparent. He was attack-
ing any feelings of sympathy or empathy that the jury might have
developed for any witness. He himself was merely interested in
the legal duties imposed on the jury, he was saying. He reminded
them that if they felt any witness had an ax to grind or was
particularly interested in the outcome, they had the right to disregard his testimony.

I felt as if the eyes of the jury focused on me. This was the
first and last time in my career that I sat in the courtroom during
the final arguments. Fortunately, the judge called a short recess,
and with Mr. Otis's okay, I left, my confidence in victory gone.
Once again, the scales seemed tipped in the other direction. It
was up to Mr. Otis in his closing argument to regain the lead.

I felt cheated that I was not in court to hear the final verbal
skirmish, since I was now deeply involved in the game known as
the adversary proceeding. But I didn't feel my presence was
beneficial. I heard later that Mr. Otis had delivered an excellent
closing argument. He had to destroy the Mark Antony gambit
("They are both honorable men") and attack Dr. Gordon personally. The prosecutor, who had the final word, in turn went
after my scalp.

The defense called for a directed verdict of not guilty by
virtue of insanity.

The prosecution asked for first degree murder.

The jury's verdict: Not guilty by virtue of insanity.

Victory belonged to the tortured, anguished Fred Lane, who
had identified so deeply with his stricken common-law wife. Fred
Lane, a shell of a man, quietly going about his duties for twenty-one
years at the same place of employment, never wanting to marry and
have children.

Hate for women? Wherever there is such deep bondage
between mother and son, there is bound to be great hate, as well
as identification. Fred Lane's self-image, his ego, had very little
chance to form. He was beaten psychologically as a boy before he
had a chance to grow into maleness. He was to be only a nurse all

his life, first to his mother, then to his sister, and finally to Maggie, his common-law wife. He dedicated his life to these three women, paying a terrible price for his dependence—the giving up of his manhood. We can only imagine the many times Fred Lane, as a child, had to give up what he wanted to do and submit passively to the wishes of his mother.

He must have grown up suffocated emotionally by the women who drained his lifeblood out of him, from whom he could not free himself. A child needs to be helped to emotional freedom. Fred Lane's mother could not help him become independent. The women he knew as a boy and later sought out as an adult would not let him call his very breath his own, psychologically.

In Fred Lane's case, we must not minimize the lack of sleep he had suffered. Deprive a man of the sleep needed "to knit the ravelled sleave of care" and he may go psychotic. The barbaric id will break through if a man is kept awake night after night, as happened to Fred Lane many years of his life because of Maggie's asthmatic fits.

In resurrecting his childhood we see the picture of a lonely, passive little boy growing up in a house where he saw only women with whom to identify. Psychologically, he had no choice, for there was no man on the scene; there was only his ailing mother, who undoubtedly hated his absent father for deserting her when she was pregnant with her third child.

When Fred Lane's mother, then his sister, died, after years of illness, he sought another ailing woman, an older woman, but the familiar woman of his life. Never did he have a chance to establish a masculine image. Masculine identity depends most on influences experienced in the first three years of life, influences arising from the mothering process. A man's development of his sexual identity occurs when he successfully starts to separate psychologically from his mother (called the separation-individuation phase of human psychosexual development), which normally occurs by the age of three. This development depends on the mother's lovingly allowing her son to grow free of her, form his own identity, as she encourages his independence and masculinity, as differentiated from her own femininity, and supports his efforts to separate from her and become an individual. Some mothers will resent and restrict their little boy's desire to be masculine, even punish him for it so that he feels that to earn his mother's love he must be passive and feminine, as she is. And somewhere along the way, Fred Lane felt that to earn his mother's love he had to nurse her when she was ill, to take care of her as his father never did, which was what he did with all the women in his life.

He had a deep identification with his mother. For courtroom purposes it would have been fruitless to go into the psychiatric concept of "identification," a psychological process that takes place naturally in every child. A child "identifies" with his mother and father, the most important people in his life, but primarily with his mother, since a baby's relationship to his mother is his first, most intense relationship. A baby believes he and his mother are one, so close is his identification (in reality, he has been one with her while in the womb). Only slowly does a baby start to differentiate between his mother and himself, and this separation continues gradually throughout childhood and adolescence. When a person matures emotionally, he is able to think of his mother and father as human beings in their own right if he has been able to separate psychologically from them.

But when there has been no father in the family, as in Fred Lane's case, a son's identification with his mother may be very deep and difficult to break free of. Since identification is accompanied by hate as well as by love, Fred Lane harbored hostility for his mother, sister and, later, Maggie Brant, a hostility he had been unable to express because his dependence on these women was so great. If it had not been, he would have been able to lead his own life, to walk away from his mother and sister and start a family of his own, and later even to walk away from Maggie, refusing to help her, thus escaping her suffering, leaving her to her daughter and doctors. But his great dependency on her kept him by her side and added to their mutual misery, a misery he eventually felt he had to end.

〰〰〰〰〰

In accordance with the Michigan law, shortly after Fred Lane was committed to the Ionia State Hospital, the institution for the criminally insane, Mr. Otis offered to file a writ of habeas corpus, but Fred Lane did not want him to do this. He wished to remain at the institution. A few years later he again refused to accept any offer to help him leave.

⬧⬧⬧⬧⬧⬧⬧⬧⬧

This case started with a telephone call, and it seems only appropriate that it ended with one, or rather, two.

A week after the conclusion of the trial, one of the jurors called my office and asked me to treat her fourteen-year-old daughter. The juror was quite disappointed when I told her I did not treat children or adolescents, but I referred her to another psychiatrist who did.

Then the day of the verdict, which was reported on the front pages of the local newspapers, the phone rang in my home. The voice of an elderly woman asked to speak to the doctor.

"I'm Dr. Tanay," I said.

She introduced herself as the widow of an eminent Detroit physician, one about whom I had heard a great deal. She said, "A number of years ago, my husband had a stroke. He was very ill, and he took a long time dying. The doctors would give him up time after time, but he kept on existing—or rather, vegetating. One night he kept trying to die but couldn't quite make it."

Her voice faded to silence. Then she said, "I could stand it no longer. I thought if I picked up a pillow and just put it over his face, it would all be ended in a few minutes."

She paused, then said, "I did just that. And you're the first person I've ever told. I felt I just had to tell you."

We talked for at least half an hour, then I thanked her for calling, knowing it had relieved her mind to confess what she had done. It was little different from Fred Lane's act that early morning of March 13, 1962. Nor from the act of many other tortured sufferers, an untold number.

It is not enough to say that the dark deeds of man have always been with us; that a man can take the life of his fellow man; that there are those among us who are fury-driven to passions they cannot endure, and who will lift the knife, the gun, the tormented hand. We must look into the darkness of their souls. We must understand that which we often do not choose to understand. We must see the shadow that is cast before.

The mask that is worn scarcely hides the nightmare thoughts that will one day turn outward in a rage of death. If we are searching for truth, we will look behind the mask, before the hidden anger erupts upon the innocent. Murder can be prevented if we look deeply into the hearts of other men and, more important, into our own.